DATE DUE			

472597

**790.1
ANT**

**The anti-boredom
book**

THE

ANTI-BOREDOM

BOOK

Magical Fun • Kitchen

Party Fun • Outdoor

Fun

Fun

THE ANTI-BOREDOM BOOK

**By the Editors of
OWL and *Chickadee* Magazines**

Edited by Marilyn Baillie and
Catherine Ripley

Owl

Contents

Party Fun

Outdoor Fun

Owl Books are published by Greey de Pencier Books Inc.
70 The Esplanade, Suite 400, Toronto, Ontario M5E 1R2

The Owl colophon is a trademark of Owl Children's Trust Inc.
Greey de Pencier Books Inc. is a licensed user of trademarks of Owl Children's Trust Inc.

Distributed in the United States by Firefly Books (U.S.) Inc.
230 Fifth Avenue, Suite 1607, New York, NY 10001

We acknowledge the financial support of the Canada Council for the Arts, the Ontario Arts
Council, and the Government of Canada through the Book Publishing Industry
Development Program (BPIDP) for our publishing activities.

Special thanks to all the past editors and art directors of OWL and *Chickadee* magazines.

The publishers would also like to thank Green Tiger Press for permission to use an idea
based on the book *Hanimals* by Mario Mariotti.

Cataloguing in Publication Data

Main entry under title:

The anti-boredom book : 133 completely unboring things to do!

Selected from: Outdoor fun, Party fun, Magical fun and Kitchen fun.
ISBN 1-894379-00-4 (bound)   ISBN 1-895688-99-X (pbk.)

1. Amusements — Juvenile literature. I. Baillie, Marilyn. II. Ripley, Catherine, 1957– .

GV1203.A57   2000   j790.1'922   C99-932371-7

Design: Wycliffe Smith, Word & Image Design Studio, Julie Colantonio

Printed in Hong Kong

B   C   D   E   F

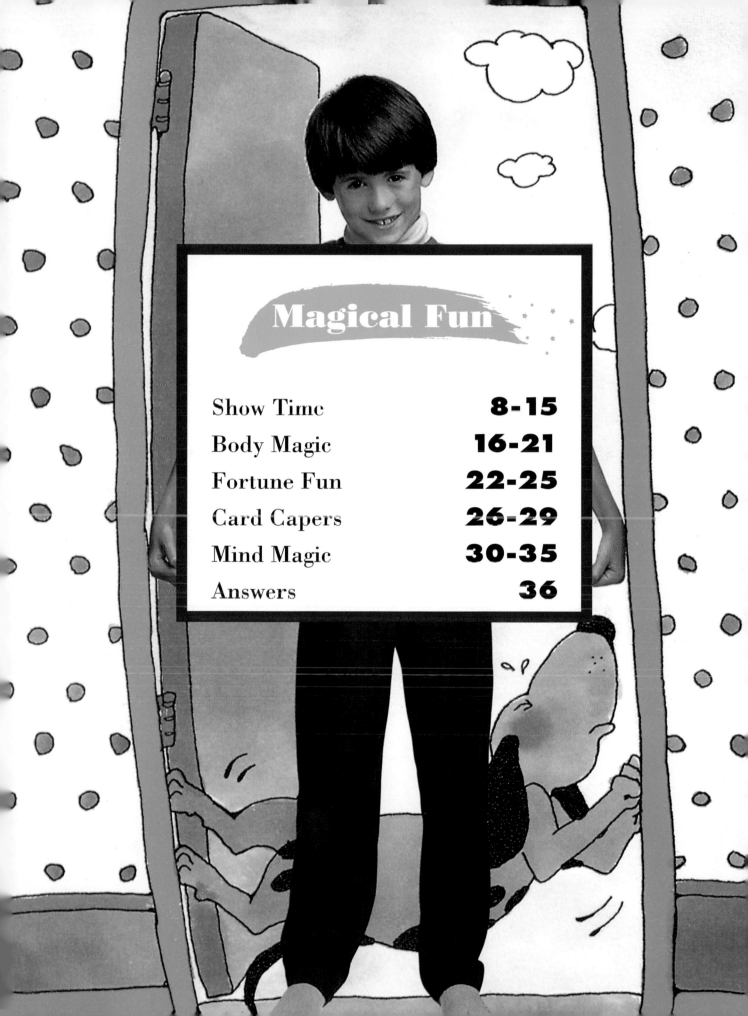

Magical Fun

Hide and Seek

Now you see it, now you don't!

DISAPPEARING PENNY TRICK

Make a coin disappear right before your friends' eyes.

You'll Need:

Old clear drinking glass
Newspaper
Construction paper
Pencil
Scissors
Glue
Coin
Scarf

The Set-up:

1. Trace around the rim of the glass on a piece of construction paper and cut out the paper circle.
2. Squeeze some glue on newspaper and dip the rim of the glass into it.
3. Place the glue-rimmed glass rim-side down on the paper circle. Let it dry.
4. Before your friends arrive, put the trick glass circle-side down on construction paper of the same color as the circle.
5. Place a coin beside the glass, and cover the trick with a scarf.
6. Practise the trick until you can do it perfectly.

The Trick:

■ Tell your friends that you are going to make a coin disappear.
■ Lift the scarf to let the audience see the glass and coin.
■ Wave the scarf with one hand in front of the glass and chant:
"Abracadabra, abracadoo.
I am amazing and so are you."
■ At the same time, quickly slide the glass over the coin with your other hand. Whip the scarf away as you shout "Ta da!" The coin "disappears"!
■ Now make the coin re-appear the same way.

Show Time

Magic Challenge 1.

Can you move one of these pennies so you make two rows of four pennies each?

See page 36 for the answer.

Paper Pranks

With a snip, snip you can slip your body
through a postcard, or fit your head through
a small paper loop.

BODY SHRINKER

**No magic potions are
needed, just the magic
touch.**

You'll Need:

2 cards, each 10 x 15 cm (4 x 8 in)
Scissors

2. With the fold towards you, make
ten cuts. Leave 1 cm (0.5 in) uncut at
the end of each cut.

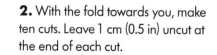

The Set-up:

1. Fold one of the cards in half the
long way.

3. Cut through all the folds, except
for the ones on each end.
4. With the folds away from you,
make more cuts between the ones
you have already made. Be careful
not to cut all the way through.

5. Open the paper carefully and
practise stepping through. Fold it up
again and put it aside.

The Trick:

■ Amaze your friends by announcing that you can fit your entire body
through a hole in a postcard.
■ Ask someone else to try it first.
Give them the scissors and an uncut
card.
■ When the trick seems too big a
task, pull out your card. Show the
audience that it is the same size as
the other. Then open up your card
and step on through.

Show Time

LOOPY LOOP

Lengthen a paper loop to twice its size without adding any more paper.

You'll Need:

Newspaper
Scissors
Clear tape

The Set-up:

1. Cut several strips of newspaper each 51 cm (20 in) long and 8 cm (3 in) wide.

2. Hold one end of a strip in each hand and bring the two ends together to form a loop. Give one end a half turn (the turn is very important) and then tape the ends together. (See picture.) Make another "magic" loop identical to this one.

The Trick:

■ Place the paper loop on your head and announce that you can magically make it fit over your head without adding paper, tape or glue.

■ Cut the loop lengthwise down the center of the strip. Everyone will be amazed to see that the loop doubles its size. Now slip it over your head.

■ Your friends will be keen to try this easy trick. Hand one of them a newspaper strip that you quickly attach but do not turn. What happens when they cut? It's not so easy.

■ Mystify your friends with more paper magic. Take a second magic loop (that you taped earlier with a half turn). This time make your cut closer to the edge than last time. Keep cutting around and around until you end up exactly where you started. Now what do you have? One loop linked to another and the other is twice as big around as the original loop. It's a loopy loop!

Mystery Box

Abracadabra! Reach right into your mystery box and magically pull things out of thin air.

You'll Need:

Cardboard shoe box with one of
    its short ends removed and saved
Scissors
Clear tape
Black paint and a paintbrush
Piece of cardboard the same length
    as the box but 5 cm (2 in) wider
Second piece of cardboard big
    enough to make a front door
    for the box
2 elastic bands
4 paper fasteners
small items

The Set-up:

1. Paint the inside of the box black and carefully cut two wide strips from the lid as shown. Tape the lid onto the box.
2. Paint both sides of the first piece of cardboard black. When dry, fold it in half the long way and slide it into the box as shown.

1

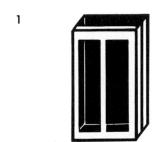

2

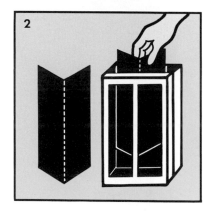

3

3. Make a front door out of the second piece of cardboard and tape it to the box. Tape the end back onto the box as a top flap.
4. Use the paper fasteners and elastic bands to make door and flap closers.
5. Before your friends arrive, stuff a few small things into the secret compartment at the rear. Close and fasten the door, then the top flap.

Show Time

The Light and Heavy Box

One famous magician astonished everyone with his magic box trick. The box was light enough for a small child to lift but it couldn't be budged by a big, muscular man. What was the secret? Under the platform the magician had placed an electromagnet! The box had a hidden metal plate. When an electric current was secretly switched on, the box stayed stuck to the platform.

The Trick:

■ Tell your friends that you can magically make objects appear from your mystery box.

■ Open the front door to show your audience that the box is empty. You can even stick your hand in to prove it.

■ Close the front door. Wave your hand over the box while you repeat a magic spell, then open the top flap.

■ "Ta da!" Pull out your hidden objects one by one.

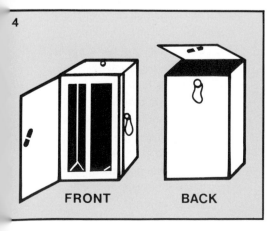

4

FRONT   BACK

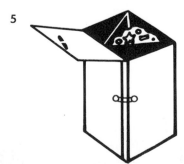

5

Mysterious Mixtures

Add mystery to your magic show with secret potions and ghostly writing.

GHOST WRITING

Fool your friends with a foggy message from a friendly ghost.

You'll Need:

Magic mix (a drop of liquid detergent in a glass with a little water)
A nearby window or a mirror

The Set-up:

1. Think of the name of a person who will be at your show. A short name works best.
2. Dip your finger into the Magic mix and print that name on a window or mirror. Let this dry so you can't see it. (If the name shows too much, add a little more water to the Magic mix and try again.)

The Trick:

■ Surprise your friends by telling them that your magical powers can make ghost writing appear. The message will probably be the name of someone at the show.
■ Mysteriously move over to the window and breathe heavily through your mouth on the invisible name. Fog will form around the printing and the name will stand out because of your Magic mix. That's really spooky!

THE WIZARD'S POTION

Make magic water fizzle and bubble at your command.

You'll Need:

Clear glass
White vinegar
Food coloring
15 ml (1 tbsp) baking soda in a bowl
Big plate or tray

The Trick:

■ Announce that you can turn plain water into a wizard's magic potion.
■ Present the glass, half filled with vinegar, and pretend it is water. Place this on a big plate or tray for the overflow.
■ Dramatically add a dash of food coloring as you mumble:
"Fizzle, fizzle, fubble,
Bibble, bibble, bubble."
■ Cast this same spell over your magic dust (baking soda) and drop the soda into the vinegar. Alakazam!
■ Now challenge someone else to try this trick but give your volunteer real water instead.

Show Time

Master of Disguise

The octopus can change color before you can say: "Abracadabra, Abracadee!" An octopus's skin is full of tiny color sacs that are controlled by muscles. The octopus can confuse its enemies by opening and closing all of these sacs so quickly that there is an instant color change. Its next trick is to disappear behind a cloud of ink. It shoots out its own black potion and makes a magic getaway behind it.

Baffling Body Tricks

All you really need is you, some friends and a little know-how.

THE HEAVY BODY TRICK
Are you heavy as a horse or light as a feather? Just move your arms a little and find out.

The Trick:

■ Tell your friends that you can make yourself so heavy that they can't possibly lift you.

■ Stand upright with your arms bent and tucked into your sides, hands at your shoulders, elbows pointing to the floor.

■ Ask two strong friends to each hold one of your elbows and lift you straight up. Up you go.

■ Tell your friends to try once more.

■ This time, before they start to lift you, place your hands securely on your shoulders and stick your elbows out to the front. This time you'll stay grounded!

Body Magic

FLOATING ARMS

Up, up and away fly your arms!

The Trick:

■ Tell a friend that you can magically raise his arms without even touching him.

■ Ask him to stand in a doorway and press the backs of his hands as hard as he can against the door frame while you count to 25.

■ Now ask him to step away from the door frame and relax. Watch out for flying arms!

PENNY PICK UP

Try to pick a penny up from this position. You will think you can but....

The Trick:

■ Challenge a friend to pick up a penny from the floor without moving his feet or bending his knees.

■ Ask him to stand with his back to the wall, feet together and heels against the wall.

■ Put a penny on the floor in front of his feet. Now watch him try!

Magic Challenge 2.

Can you pick up an empty soda pop bottle using only a straw? Don't touch the bottle with your hands.

See page 36 for the answer.

Tricky Fingers

Here are a few handy tricks to have up your sleeve.

TWIST AND TIE

Here's how to cross your arms and tie a knot...all in one!

The Set-up:

1. Lay a scarf lengthwise in front of you, on a table.
2. Fold your arms.
3. Grasp one end of the scarf with your hand that is up and the other end with the hand that is down.
4. Firmly hold the scarf and unfold your arms. Now you have a knot in the middle.

The Trick:

■ Place the scarf in front of a friend. Ask her to fold her arms and then tie a knot. Chances are she will try but will not be able to tie the knot.
■ Now it is your turn to show your super duper knot-tying powers.

Body Magic

FINGER TWIST

SHAZAM! With one magic word you can make a friend's fingers do funny things.

The Set-up:

1. Your friend should interlock his fingers as shown.

The Trick:

■ Cast the magic spell and inform your friend that he no longer has control over his fingers.
■ Without touching him, point to one of his fingers and ask him to move it. He'll move any finger but the correct one.

Baby Fingers

Put your finger in the hand of a baby and she or he will grab on tightly. Why do their tiny fingers seem to grasp at everything? Babies can't help themselves. They are always looking for warmth and love or food. Their busy fingers keep them in touch with people who love them.

BROKEN THUMB

Thumbs up to the magician who can split a thumb in two and then magically make it one again.

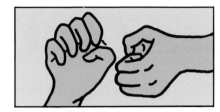

The Set-up:

1. Place your left hand against your waist, palm up and thumb on the outside. Now bend both your thumbs and bring them together in front of you, knuckle to knuckle. Your right thumb should look like an extension of your left thumb. (See drawing.)

2. Hide the crack where the two thumbs join with your right index finger.

3. Keep your index finger in front as a screen and move your right hand to the right to separate your thumbs.

You must practise this in front of a mirror many times before your show. Then it will seem easy.

The Trick:

■ Amaze your audience by announcing that you can break your thumb in two.
■ Face your audience, place your thumbs and index finger in position, and slowly work your magic. This quick and easy trick can be done any time and your friends will love it.

H.C. STORM SCHOOL

Eye Puzzlers

You have to keep an eye on these puzzles!
They'll trick your eyes and fool your brain.

Table Top Trick

Can you fit a penny on top of this table without touching the sides? Try it and find out.

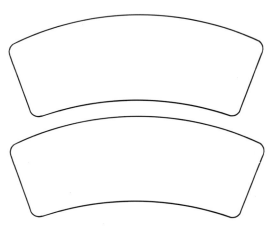

Mystifying Shapes

Which shape is larger?

Puzzling Pattern

What happens to the pattern when you stare at it?

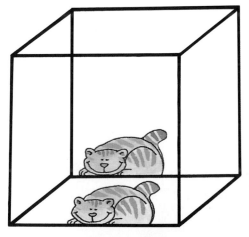

Crazy Cats

Stare at the cube for several seconds. Which cat is closer?

Body Magic

Disappearing Diamond

Try this trick to solve the mystery of the missing diamond.

The Trick:

■ Hold the two of diamonds at arm's length in front of you.

■ Close your left eye. Stare at the diamond on the left with your right eye.

■ Move the card very slowly towards you and keep looking at the diamond on the left.

■ Suddenly, the diamond on the right will vanish. Move the card away from you and you'll find the missing diamond again!

Magic Challenge 3.

Can you add five lines to these six to make nine?

See page 36 for the answer.

Fantastic Fortune Cake

Bake a chocolate chip Fortune Cake and invite your friends to munch away to find their fortunes.

You'll Need:

125 mL (1/2 cup) butter
250 mL (1 cup) white sugar
2 eggs
5 mL (1 tsp) vanilla
5 mL (1 tsp) baking soda
5 mL (1 tsp) baking powder
250 mL (1 cup) sour cream or yogurt
500 mL (2 cups) flour
500 mL (2 cups) chocolate chips
Mixing bowls, measuring cups and spoons
Greased angel cake pan
Paper
Waxed paper
Oven preheated to 175°C (350°F)
   (Ask an adult to help you.)

3 is your lucky number

Something exciting will happen today

Here's How:

■ Make your cake following these steps. Cream together the butter and sugar. Add other ingredients in the order listed and mix well with a spoon. Pour into the greased angel cake pan. Bake for 40 to 45 minutes. Cool and place on a dish.

Fortune Fun

Something exciting will happen today!

Wonder Powder

Baking soda is the "magic" ingredient that made your cake rise. Here are some other amazing things it can do:
- **Shine some silver**
- **Scrub a sink**
- **Refresh a refrigerator**
- **Remove a carpet stain**
- **And even clean your teeth!**

■ Cut small up-and-down slits around the outside of the cake so each fortune will have a secret slot.

■ Write fortunes on small pieces of paper and wrap each in waxed paper.

■ Slip a fortune into every slot. Then ice the cake with your favorite icing.

■ Now celebrate the end of your show with a big surprise!

MYSTIC MUFFINS

Mystic Muffins are great for magicians on the move. Take them on a trip or tuck them in your lunch box. They'll be a treat wherever you go!

Here's How:

■ Follow your favorite muffin recipe or make the recipe on page 18.

■ Line a muffin pan with paper cupcake holders.

■ Put a wrapped-up fortune in each paper holder.

■ Pour in the muffin mix and bake.

Fast Fortune Flicker

Who needs a crystal ball? Become a fortune teller by making your very own Fortune Flicker.

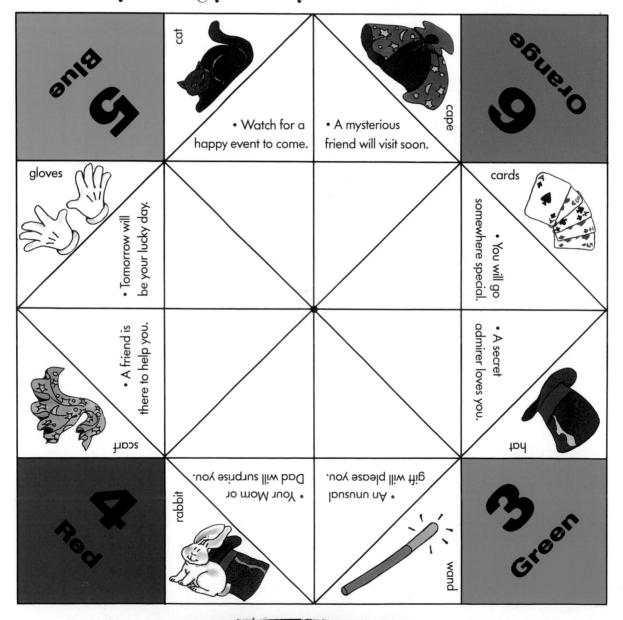

Blue 5

cat

• Watch for a happy event to come.

• A mysterious friend will visit soon.

cape

Orange 6

gloves

• Tomorrow will be your lucky day.

• You will go somewhere special.

cards

• A friend is there to help you.

• A secret admirer loves you.

scarf

hat

Red 4

rabbit

• Your Mom or Dad will surprise you.

• An unusual gift will please you.

wand

Green 3

Fortune Fun

How To Play It

1. Place your fingers and thumbs in your Fortune Flicker. Ask a friend to choose one of the squares.

2. Spell the color or count the number of the chosen square and, for each count or letter, open or close the flicker. Leave it open on the last letter or number.

3. Ask your friend to choose one of the objects shown in the center of the flicker.

4. Spell the word or count the number out loud. Open and close the flicker as you did the first time.

5. Ask your friend to choose another object.

6. Unfold the flap of the object chosen and read the fortune.

How To Make It

1. Trace the pattern and lines shown here onto a square piece of paper. Write in the fortunes, color the squares and draw the objects.

2. Turn the square over and trace the centre dot onto that blank side. Fold each of the four corners in to the new centre dot.

3. Turn back over and again fold all four new corners in to the centre.

4. Now fold the square in half in one direction, then unfold and fold in half in the other direction.

5. Slip your index finger and thumb of each hand under the four colored flaps. Squeeze your thumbs and fingers together. Open and close the flicker by separating your fingers and thumbs first sideways and then back-to-front.

Superstitious?

You're walking along the street and a black cat crosses in front of you. Is this a sign of good or bad luck? In parts of North America, a black cat is thought to bring bad luck. In England, Japan and parts of Europe, however, seeing a black cat means good fortune will come your way!

The 1, 2, 3 Card Trick

Presto, find-o, alamazoo!
The card turns up each time for you.

The Trick:

■ Chant mysteriously to your friends, "Presto, find-o, alamazoo! I'm sure to find the card for you."

1. Count out 21 cards from a deck. Place them face down, in three piles of seven cards each.

2. Pick up one of the piles of cards in front of you. Fan the seven cards out face up so everyone can see them.

3. Ask someone to mentally choose a card and remember it. (He or she may tell the rest of the audience but the magician must not know.)

4. Put the card piles back together, placing the pile with the secret card in between the other two piles.

5. Deal the cards face up in three piles of seven cards each. Be sure to move from left to right, putting one card on each pile each time you deal.

6. Ask the friend to point to the pile that contains the secret card.

7. Gather the cards up again, carefully keeping the pile with the secret card between the other two.

8. Deal the cards into a single pile but as you pick up each card pretend you are weighing it to receive the magic vibrations. Count the cards silently. Then "Ta da!" Show the secret card. It will always be the eleventh one.

Magic Challenge 4.

Line up six glasses and fill the first three with water. Now move just one glass so that the pattern of glasses is full, empty, full, empty, full, empty.

| 1 | 2 | 3 | 4 | 5 | 6 |

See page 36 for the answer.

Card Capers

Check the Deck

Collect card tricks. Show them in your magic show or keep them for a rainy day.

WHERE'S JACK?

Who can find the Jack?

You'll Need:

The Jack and three other cards from an old deck of cards
Scissors
Glue

The Set-up:

1. Cut the Jack from the bottom left corner to the middle at the top of the card. (See picture.)
2. Glue the left piece from the Jack at an angle across the face of another card.
3. Carefully arrange the two remaining cards on top of each other and treat them as one.
4. Now place these two cards partly over the Jack so the Jack is just peeking out. (See picture.) You are holding three cards but only two can be seen along with the fake Jack.

The Trick:

■ Hold up the cards with the Jack in the middle. Tell a long story about Jack and how he often disappears. Ask everyone to keep an eye on him.

■ Close the cards. Turn them upside-down (not around) to face you. Fan them out. Jack should be gone.
■ Invite someone to point to the back of the card they think is Jack. But when you turn the cards to face them, Jack isn't there at all!

Card Capers

28

THE BLACK AND RED TRICK

This trick is quick and easy but your friends will never guess the secret.

The Trick:

■ Before you start the trick, fix your deck. Pile all the red cards at one end of the deck and the black ones at the other.

■ Turn the deck face down. Fan out the red cards and keep the black ones tucked at the bottom of the deck.

■ Ask a friend to pull a card out, look at it and remember it.

■ Meanwhile, close the deck in your hand. Fan the cards out again (still face down) but this time fan out the black cards.

■ Tell your friend to put the card back in the deck.

■ Look mysteriously through the deck and you will easily find the one red card among the black ones. Pretend that your magic powers have guided you to the secret card.

Playing Cards

Take a good look at the clothes on the Queen and King in your deck. They're wearing the court costume of King Henry VII of England. He lived over four hundred years ago. And playing cards have been around even longer than that! There are hundreds of different card games, and some people even "tell fortunes" with cards.

29

Mind Reading

"Mirror, mirror on the wall,
Who is the best magician of all?"

Try this amazing, mind-boggling trick and the answer might be "You!"

Number Telepathy

A whiz kid and a mind reader, too? Test your numbers know-how with this trick.

The Set-up:

1. Practise with a partner the secret sign you will use to pass the correct number along.
2. Gently place your hands on each side of your partner's head. Your fingers should be over his ears and your palms covering the back of his jaw.

3. Now your partner makes short chewing motions with his teeth together and his mouth closed. You can feel it but others can't see it.
4. Count the number of "chews" and you will have the answer. If he "chews" ten times, the number is ten.

Magic Challenge 5.

Pick a number. Now double it and add five. Add twelve. Take away three. Now halve it. Take away the number you first picked. What will the answer always be?

See page 36 for the answer.

The Trick:

■ Who will believe that a Master Magician can feel numbers right through people's heads?
■ Ask your friends to decide, while you are out of the room, on a number between one and ten.
■ When you return, move mysteriously about the room, feeling people's heads and faces. It takes a few minutes for you to feel the right impulses from the brain.
■ Your partner gives you the correct number with your secret sign. Once again you prove to be the one and only, the amazing Master Magician!

Mind Magic

Magic Messages

Try these tricks, then think up some more for your magic message box.

THE KNOW-IT-ALL BOX

You'll pick the right answer from this box every time.

You'll Need:

A big cardboard box
Bright wrapping paper
Colored or shiny paper
Paints
Glue or clear tape
Scissors
An envelope
Pencil and small pieces of paper

The Set-up:

1. Cover your box with bright paper. Decorate it with colored-paper cut-outs or paints.

2. Draw a picture of a dog on a piece of paper and write the word "dog" underneath it. Stuff this in an envelope and seal it.

The Trick:

■ Tell your audience that inside the sealed envelope is the name of an animal and announce that your Know-it-all Box will be able to figure out what that animal is.

■ Ask your audience to help by naming some animals for you to write on the small pieces of paper and put into the box.

■ Chances are that someone will call out "dog", but if you want to be doubly sure, plant a friend in the audience to say it.

Mind Magic

■ The trick is to write "dog," instead of the audience's suggestions, on every piece of paper!

■ Chant: "Hocus Pocus, Jimminy Occus," and wave your hands in the air. Swoop down and pull out a name from the box. It's "dog!"

■ Now the tension mounts. Open the sealed envelope and…Surprise! The Know-it-all Box knows all.

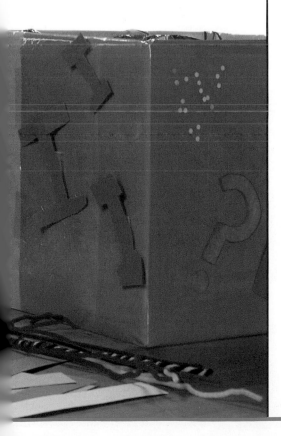

COLOR VISION

This famous trick is for the magician with eyes in the back of her head.

You'll Need:

The Know-it-all Box
Box of crayons

The Set-up:

Place the Know-it-all Box in front of you and dump the crayons inside.

The Trick:

■ Casually announce that you can see color through the eyes in the back of your head.

■ Turn your back to the audience. Ask a volunteer to show everyone the crayons in the box and then choose one.

■ Direct her to place the crayon in your hands which are held behind your back.

■ As you turn around to face the audience, secretly dig one finger- or thumbnail into the crayon.

■ Keep the crayon behind your back in one hand. Bring the other hand forward - the one with the crayon bits under your nail.

■ Pretend you are trying to "see" through the back of your head and move your free hand up to your forehead. Meanwhile, have a peek at the color on your nail.

■ Suddenly, you are struck with a color vision and you magically call out the color. It's true! Magicians do have eyes in the back of their heads.

Trick Tips

Whether you want to put on a full magic show or just impress your friends and family, these tips will help make your performance even more impressive.

1. Practise, practise, practise! Try your tricks in front of a mirror.

2. Never tell how a trick is done and never do a trick twice. You'll lose the magic of it all.

3. Mix your tricks so your audience is surprised with a variety of magic. You might move from a card trick to mind reading to a vanishing coin trick.

Abracadabra

"Abracadabra" is a very, very old magical charm. In the ancient Orient people thought that chanting this special word would bring help from kind spirits to ward off sickness. Through the Middle Ages, "Abracadabra" became used more generally in magic. Chant it when you do some of your more mysterious tricks.

Mind Magic

4. Find a table for your show and cover it with a cloth that reaches down to the ground.

5. Set up your tricks well in advance with your supplies arranged under the table ready to be used.

7. Keep your audience in front of your table, not to the sides.

8. Be sure to look at your audience and speak clearly. This is your show!

6. Use hand gestures to distract or add to the drama. Frown, pause, stare or chit-chat to set the magic tone. Remember, you are the actor.

9. Start your act with a trick that is quick and exciting. End your performance with your best trick.

10. Learn some jokes to fill in the time between tricks.

11. Use special effects to set a magical mood. Blow bubbles or dried dandelions around for friends to catch and make magic wishes on.

DISAPPEARING PENNY TRICK

12. Have lots of fun!

Answers

Eye Puzzlers

Table Top Trick

The penny won't fit because the picture of a table is a parallelogram, not a rectangle as a real table is.

Crazy Cats

If you look at the cube long enough, each cat seems to take a turn being closer than the other.

Mystifying Shape

Both are exactly the same size.

Puzzling Patterns

The pattern appears to vibrate.

Challenges

Magic Challenge 1.

Place the penny on the right on top of the middle one.

Magic Challenge 2.

Bend the straw about three quarters of the way down. Push the bent end

into the empty soda bottle. Make sure the bent straw is pressing against the inside of the bottle. Now hold the long end of the straw and carefully lift the bottle. Ta da!

Magic Challenge 3.

Magic Challenge 4.

Pick up glass 2 and pour the water from it into glass 5. Then return glass 2 to its place.

Magic Challenge 5.

The answer is always seven!

Kitchen Fun

Wacky Walnuts

Save those walnut shells!
They turn into fabulous fridge magnets
and make great gifts, too.

You'll Need:

Cleaned-out walnut halves (*Ask an adult to slide a screwdriver down the middle of the nuts to split them.*)
Poster paint
Clear nail polish
White glue
Scissors
Decorating materials (pasta, pipe cleaners, colored paper...)
Felt or construction paper
Magnetic tape (found in craft stores)

Here's How:

■ Paint the shells. When dry, put on a coat of clear nail polish.
■ Add eyes, ears, whiskers or tails with your decorating materials.

■ Cut a piece of felt to fit the bottom of the shell and glue in place.
■ Now paste a piece of magnetic tape to the felt, and your fridge magnet is ready to stick up.

Fortune Nuts

Make a bunch of fortune nuts for your friends and see who chooses which future. Ask an adult to split the walnuts down the middle with a screwdriver. Clean out the nut meat. Then pop in fortunes written on strips of paper. Stick the walnuts back together using white glue.

Leftover Art

Beaumark

at do
call a
lnut
t sticks
the
idge?

A
magNUT,
of course!!

Is a peanut a nut?

No! A peanut is not a nut, and it doesn't grow on a tree. Instead it is a legume, a member of the pea and bean family, and surprisingly, it grows underground.

Peanut Puppets

Don't throw out those peanut shells just yet! They can turn into great puppets. Put a funny face on each half with a marker, and pop them on your fingers. Then let your fingers do the talking!

Bird Eggs-travaganza

**Wait! Don't crack that egg!
Instead blow the inside out, save the shell
and transform it into a very
"tweet" bird.**

You'll Need:

Raw eggs
Pin or thick needle
Bowls
Food coloring
Decorating materials (markers, paints, pipe cleaners, construction paper...)
Brightly colored embroidery thread or wool

Here's How:

■ Ask an adult to help you tap the pin into the small end of an egg.
■ Now make a bigger hole in the other end.
■ Blow through the small hole and watch the insides come out the other end into a bowl.

■ When you've blown several eggs, scramble up the insides for a meal.
■ Wash the shells carefully and dry.

■ Dip the eggs in bowls of food coloring mixed with water and let them sit for a few minutes.
■ Remove and let dry.

■ Place each egg on its side and start adding bird decorations (construction paper wings and beak, marker or split-pea eyes, pipe-cleaner feet).
■ Thread the wool through the small hole with a long needle and pull through the other end. Tie a knot to complete your hanging loop.
■ Hang the birdies from twigs in a table vase or let them fly from a mobile. How tweet!

Who lays the largest egg in the world?

An ostrich! One ostrich egg weighs as much as two dozen chicken eggs.

Build with Bones

This dinosaur looks as though it belongs in a museum, but it's made from chicken bones!

You'll Need:

Chicken carcass
Pot filled with water

Cookie sheet
White glue
Modelling clay
Heavy paper

Leftover Art

Here's How:

(*Ask an adult for help.*)

■ Boil the bones for 30 minutes.
■ When the bones are cool enough to touch, scrape the bones clean. The leftover chicken meat and water are a good start for homemade soup.

■ Bake the bones in the oven at a low temperature for 30 minutes.
■ Now design a dinosaur. White glue works best for sticking the bones on paper, and modelling clay holds the bones together well.

■ The bird's breastbone makes a perfect pterodactyl, one of the huge flying reptiles from dinosaur days.

Kitchen Challenge 1.

How can you make a chicken bone bend?

See page 66 for the answer.

Ta Da!

Amaze your friends with some everyday magic.
All you need are a few things from your kitchen cupboards.

SPOON TRICK

Test your sense of balance by doing this spoon trick.

Here's How:

■ Hold the spoon with the handle down.
■ Place the bowl over the tip of your nose.
■ When you sense that the spoon is balancing by itself, let go. Ta da!

Why?
Just like the spoon, every object has a balancing point. What else can you balance on your body?

KNIFE TRICK

Pick up a heavy jar of rice with only a knife.

Here's How:

(Ask an adult for help.)

■ Work over a table or counter at all times while doing this trick.
■ Fill a narrow-necked jar with uncooked rice.
■ Jab a serated or plain steel knife about 2.5 cm (1 inch) into the rice over and over again for a minute.
■ Now plunge the knife deep into the rice and lift carefully. Ta da!

Why?
Friction is strong! It is the friction between the tightly packed rice and the knife that lets you lift the jar.

WATER TRICK

How can you float a cork in a glass of water so it doesn't touch the sides?

Here's How:

■ Slowly fill a glass with water so the top bulges up into a dome.
■ Place the cork in the middle of the dome. Ta da!

Why?
The cork is lighter than the water so it floats at the highest point of the water dome. What else will float here?

Kitchen Challenge 2.

How can you make a single sheet of paper hold up a heavy cookbook?

See page 66 for the answer.

Presto!

Volcano Countdown

**Make a volcano erupt
on your very own kitchen table.**

You'll Need:

Empty flower pot placed upside
  down in a large, deep baking
  pan
Empty tuna tin with one end
  removed
Plastic or paper cup with the
  bottom cut off, upside down on
  the tin (*Pull the sides of the
  cup together tightly around the
  tin and tape. You may have to
  cut a small v in the side of the
  cup to make it fit snugly.*)
Scissors
Masking tape
Tinfoil
Spoons
125 mL (1/2 cup) vinegar
Baking soda
Red food coloring or powdered
  paint
Dish soap

Here's How:

■ Put the tin and paper cup on
top of the flower pot.
■ Cover your ''mountain'' with
tinfoil and crinkle it.
■ Cut an X on top of the foil and
fold it down inside the cup to
make a hole.

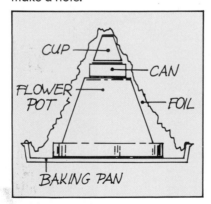

■ Add a spoonful of baking soda
and a spoonful of dish soap to the
tin through the hole.
■ Measure out the vinegar and
add a spoonful of food coloring.

■ Start your volcano countdown
as you pour the vinegar through
the hole. Presto!

Volcanoes even erupt underwater!

**Deep-sea volcanoes
are mountain makers,
and in places, island
makers. Iceland is one
island that was made
by volcanoes. Watch
for the next volcano
to rise from the depths
of the sea. It's scheduled
to appear in the
Caribbean in the year
2000 and will be
called Kick'em Jenny.**

Presto!

Incredible Cookies

Make three amazing types of cookies— all from one basic recipe.

You'll Need:

250 mL (1 cup) brown sugar,
   125 mL (¹/₂ cup) margarine,
   1 egg, 5 mL (1 tsp) vanilla
   (*Beat these ingredients
   together first.*)
300 mL (1¹/₄ cup) flour, 2 mL
   (¹/₂ tsp) baking powder,
   2 mL (¹/₂ tsp) salt (*Mix these
   ingredients together and then
   add to the margarine
   mixture.*)
Mixing bowls, spoons, greased
   cookie sheets
Preheated oven
(*Ask an adult for help.*)

RAINBOW GLASS COOKIES

Extra ingredients: about 250 mL
   (1 cup) extra flour, tinfoil,
   smashed clear candies (*Ask an
   adult to help you smash them,
   one color at a time, with a
   hammer between waxed
   paper.*)
Oven temperature: 160°C
   (325°F)

■ Add the extra flour until the dough feels like soft clay. If it's too dry, add a little water.
■ Chill the dough for 20 minutes in the freezer.
■ Roll out dough snakes on a flat surface.
■ Make designs with the snakes on a foil-lined cookie sheet. Press the ends of each shape together with your fingers.
■ Bake the cookies for about 5 minutes—don't let them brown!
■ Ask an adult to help you take the cookies out of the oven.
■ Fill each shape with an even layer of smashed candies. Watch out—the pan will be hot.

■ Put them back in the oven. In about 5 minutes, the candy will start to bubble. Remove the pan.
■ Cool the cookies for about 30 minutes. Then pull the foil off the back of the cookies. Hang them in a cool place for decoration or eat them. Mmmm!

Which bitter beans turn into a sweet and scrumptious treat?

Cocoa beans, of course! They grow in the hottest part of the world. Before they get to you in your local store as chocolate, they are picked, fermented, dried, roasted, crushed, cooled, pressed, kneaded, heated and again cooled!

Digging into Dough

COOKIE POPS

Extra ingredients: chocolate chips, wooden ice cream sticks, food coloring (optional), waxed paper
Oven temperature: 200°C (400°F)

■ Wrap the dough mixture in waxed paper and refrigerate one hour.
■ Make thin dough sandwiches with chocolate chips inside and seal the edges.

■ Push a wooden stick into each one and bake on a cookie sheet for 8 minutes.
■ Be sure to let the pops cool completely before lifting off the cookie sheet.

Feeling sad?

Eat chocolate! It causes certain glands in your body to secrete hormones that make you feel happier.

GIFT BOX

Extra ingredients: 175 mL (³/₄ cup) chocolate chips, a greased tinfoil pattern scaled up from the one given.
Oven temperature: 175°C (350°F)

■ Add 125 mL (¹/₂ cup) of the chocolate chips to your dough mixture.
■ Carefully pat out the dough to fill the tinfoil shapes, until it is about 1 cm (³/₈ inch) thick.

Scale these up to whatever size you like

Top cut 1

Side cut 2

Bot. cut 1

Ends cut 2

■ Place the shapes on a cookie sheet and bake in the oven for about 10 minutes.
■ Ask an adult to help you melt the rest of the chocolate chips over hot water.
■ Glue your box together with the melted chocolate and support the sides until the "glue" sets.

Pass the Pizza

What's this? Tiny fish pizzas?
What about face pizzas? Stop sign pizzas? House pizzas?
The sky's the limit—just don't make it round!

You'll Need:

500 mL (2 cups) flour, 10 mL
(2 tsp) baking powder, 2 mL
(¹/₂ tsp) salt (*Mix together in a
bowl.*)
50 mL (¹/₄ cup) olive oil, 50 mL
(¹/₄ cup) milk, 2 eggs (*Mix
together, add to dry
ingredients and stir until
dough is stiff.*)
Spaghetti sauce
Your favorite pizza toppings
(pepperoni, green pepper,
pineapple, mushrooms,
olives…)
Bowls, wooden spoon, rolling pin,
greased cookie sheet
Oven preheated to 190°C
(375°F) (*Ask an adult to help.*)

Here's How:

■ When all of the flour has
disappeared in the dough
mixture, put it out on a counter
sprinkled with flour.
■ Rub flour on the rolling pin and
roll the dough out until it's .5 cm
(¹/₄ inch) thick.
■ Shape and cut the dough into
any shape you want and then
carefully place it on the cookie
sheet.
■ Spoon on a thin layer of the
spaghetti sauce.
■ Add the toppings to complete
your design.
■ Bake the pizzas—about 18
minutes for smaller ones or 25
minutes for one large one.

Who invented pizza?

**The Greeks did—
almost three thousand
years ago! The first
pizzas were simple,
made from local flour,
olive oil, olives, herbs
and cheeses. It wasn't
until the 1800s that
the rest of the world
began to catch on to
the idea of pizza, the
perfect plate—one
you eat instead of
wash!**

Digging into Dough

Sourdough Surprise

**Here's a cake with a pioneering heart!
It's based on a yeast starter that has been passed down
to us from the early settlers of North America.**

START SOME STARTER

You'll Need:

500 mL (2 cups) warm water
1 pkg. active dry yeast
15 mL (1 tbsp) sugar
500 mL (2 cups) all-purpose flour
Glass bowl
Wooden spoon
Clean cloth

Here's How:

■ Mix up the starter ingredients.
■ Cover with the cloth and place
in a warm, draft-free place for
about 6 hours.

■ Store the starter in a plastic
container in the fridge until ready
to make your cake or give some
away.

■ If you want to share your
starter with friends, give them
plastic containers with the starter
inside and tags that read:
Store me in the fridge and feed
me equal amounts of water and
flour every 7-10 days. After you
feed me, let me stand at room
temperature overnight. Then use
some of me to make a sourdough
cake and pass on the rest.

Listen! Can you hear the starter growing?

**The yeast in the
starter is a type of
fungus that multiplies
quickly when given
warm water and
sugar to feed on. As
the yeast grows, it
produces noisy
bubbles of carbon
dioxide.**

Digging into Dough

SOURDOUGH CHOCOLATE CAKE

You'll Need:

250 mL (1 cup) margarine,
500 mL (2 cups) sugar, 2 eggs,
5 mL (1 tsp) vanilla, 250 mL
(1 cup) sourdough starter,
100 mL (¹/₃ cup) milk (*Blend
ingredients together in the
order listed*.)

500 mL (2 cups) all-purpose flour,
5 mL (1 tsp) baking soda,
175 mL (²/₃ cup) unsweetened
cocoa (*Mix together well*.)
Icing
Mixing bowls, measuring cups,
spoons
20 cm (8 inch) greased round
cake pan
20 cm (8 inch) greased square
cake pan
Oven preheated to 175°C
(350°F) (*Ask an adult*.)

Here's How:

■ Add the dry ingredients to the
"wet" ones and stir well.
■ Pour half the batter into each
pan and bake for 30-40 minutes.
■ Cool the cakes on racks.
■ Then cut and assemble the
cakes as shown in the pattern.
■ Ice with your favorite icing.

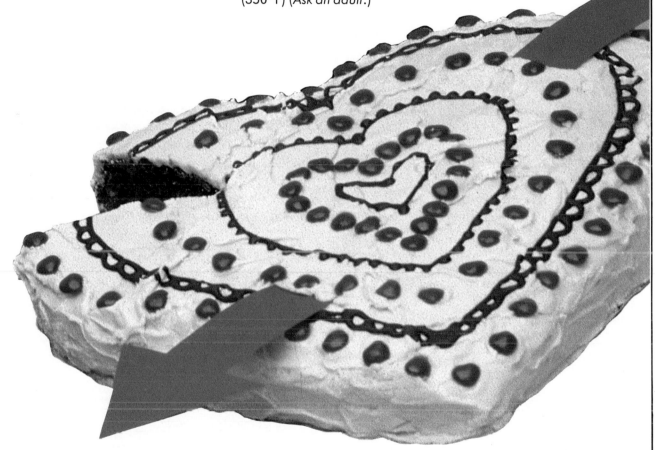

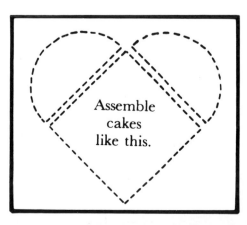

Assemble
cakes
like this.

Perfect Pretzels

If your lunches are ho-hum, pack a pretzel into your brown bag for a pick-me-up change.

You'll Need:

250 mL (1 cup) warm water,
 15 mL (1 tbsp) dry yeast, 15 mL
 (1 tbsp) honey (*Mix together in
 a bowl, set it in a warm place
 for 10 minutes or until yeast is
 bubbling.*)
15 mL (1 tbsp) oil
5 mL (1 tsp) salt
250 mL (1 cup) whole wheat flour
625 mL (2 1/2 cups) all-purpose
 flour
Egg white
Mixing bowl, measuring cup and
 spoons, clean damp cloth,
 wooden spoon, rolling pin,
 knife, cookie sheet

Here's How:

■ Stir the oil and salt into the yeast mixture, and little by little, add the flour.
■ When the dough is too stiff to stir, put it on a floured counter.
■ Knead it well by punching the middle of the dough and folding in the sides.
■ Punch and fold for about 10 minutes or until the dough is smooth and stretchy.
■ Put the dough into a clean, greased bowl, cover it with the cloth and place in a warm place for an hour.
■ When the dough has risen to twice its original size, you can start pretzelling.
■ First ask an adult to preheat the oven to 200°C (400°F).
■ Roll out the dough on a clean surface until it is 2 cm (1/2 inch) thick and cut into thin strips.

■ Make dough snakes and shape into letters or animals or whatever you like.
■ Place the shapes on a cookie sheet and paint with egg white.
■ Bake until golden brown, about 8-10 minutes.

Kitchen Challenge 3.

How can a pretzel turn iodine from red to black?

Turn to page 66 for the answer.

Digging into Dough

Ice is Nice

Use your freezer to transform juice and water to super ice surprises. MMMMMM good!

ICE PUPPETS

Make some neat ice puppets and then slurp them up for a cool treat.

You'll Need:

Plastic baby food containers or yogurt containers

Wooden ice cream sticks

Icing paste (*Drip cold water slowly into 30 mL (2 tbsp) icing sugar until thick and sticky.*)

Face decorations (raisins, orange pieces, chocolate chips, assorted berries…)

Skirts (tinfoil or cloth squares)

Paper towels or napkins

Here's How:

■ Dip your finger in the icing paste and draw a face on the inside of the container. Then press the face decorations firmly into place in the icing paste. (See illustration 1.)

■ Secure the wooden stick to the bottom of the container with a big blob of icing paste. (See illustration 2.) Freeze container for about ½ hour or until icing is frozen.

■ Remove from freezer and fill the container with your favorite juice. Put container back into freezer for a couple of hours, or until frozen.

■ When you take the container out, run warm water over it to loosen the ice from the sides.

■ Before sliding the puppet out, poke the skirt over the wooden stick so it is resting at the base of the puppet face.

■ Add several petticoats of paper towel to protect your hand from the cold.

■ With your hand under the skirt, hold onto the wooden stick and turn the puppet over. Pull the container off and get ready to perform! (See illustration 3.)

Banana Bonanza

For a cool treat, peel a banana, wrap it in foil and place it in the freezer for a couple of hours.

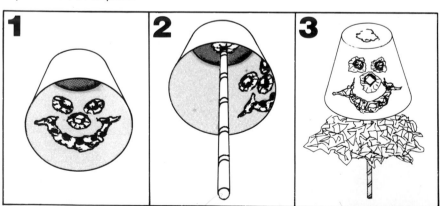

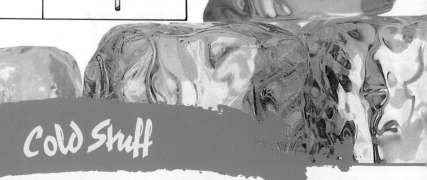

Cold Stuff

COOL CUBES

Make up some ice cubes with class for your long, cold drinks.

You'll Need:

Ice cube tray
Fruit pieces (*Berries, melon balls, and orange slices work well.*)
Water or fruit juice

Here's How:

■ Drop the fruit pieces into each section of the ice cube tray.
■ Fill the tray with water or juice and freeze.
■ Add the cubes to cold drinks for a tasty treat.

Kitchen Challenge 4.

How can you make an ice cube somersault?

See page 66 for the answer.

Ice Cream Magic

Nothing beats ice cream for a cool and frosty snack.
Try out these recipes for ice cream with pizzazz.

ICE CREAM CUPS

Make a cup of good old-fashioned soft ice cream, using salt and ice!

You'll Need:

375 mL (1 1/2 cups) crushed ice
125 mL (1/2 cup) salt
125 mL (1/2 cup) whipping cream
50 mL (1/4 cup) sugar
1 mL (1/4 tsp) vanilla
Small paper cup
Styrofoam cup (large enough for the paper one to fit inside)
Wooden ice cream stick
Plastic wrap
Elastic

Here's How:

■ Mix the cream, vanilla and sugar together in the paper cup.
■ Use the elastic to fasten the plastic wrap in place over the paper cup.
■ Mix the salt and ice together in the styrofoam cup.
■ Place the paper cup into the bigger cup so that the ice and salt mixture surrounds it.
■ Now remove the plastic wrap. Be careful not to get any salty ice into your ice cream.
■ Stir the cream mixture off and on for the next 15 to 20 minutes. By then you'll have delicious soft ice cream to taste!

Pass the Spoons

In 1985 the largest ice cream sundae ever to be made was served up at the Disneyland Hotel in Anaheim, California. Want to beat this record? You'd have to gather together enough ice cream to almost equal the weight of 2 elephants, add just over 25 bathtubs of topping and end with 15 pails of whipping cream!

Cold Stuff

WONDERFUL WATERMELON

This watermelon wasn't grown on a vine—it's made of ice cream! Make it in the morning and eat it for dessert at dinnertime.

You'll Need:

1 L (4 cups) green ice cream
1 L (4 cups) pink ice cream
125 mL (½ cup) chocolate chips
Large bowl lined with tinfoil
Spoon
Alarm clock (*Set the alarm for the times mentioned.*)
Platter

Here's How:

■ Chill the bowl for 30 minutes in the freezer.
■ Shape a layer of green ice cream around the inside of the bowl to a depth of your thumb.
■ Put the bowl back in the freezer.
■ After 3 hours, start softening the pink ice cream until you can stir in the chocolate chips. Spoon the mixture into the bowl. Freeze until firm, about 3 more hours.
■ When it's time for dessert, turn the bowl upside down on a plate and remove bowl and foil. Mmmmmmmmm!

Crazy Cans

Collect cans of all shapes and sizes.
Then make the games you see here
and have a crazy can afternoon of fun.

STRUTTING ON STILTS

Walk tall on a pair of juice cans.

You'll Need:

2 large, empty juice cans with a
hole punched on each side
near the top (*Ask an adult to
make these holes with a
hammer and nail.*)

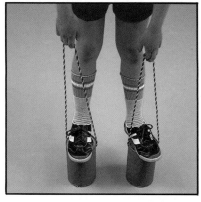

2 pieces of rope (long enough to
loop through the holes and up
to your hands when you stand
on the cans)

Here's How:

■ Thread the rope through the
holes in each can.
■ Tie a knot so that you can
hold the rope in your hands
comfortably when you stand on
the cans.
■ Now pull the ropes tight and
away you strut!

TELEPHONE TALK

**Believe it or not, you can talk
to a friend through a tin can!**

You'll Need:

2 tin cans with holes punched in
the bottom (*Ask an adult to
help you use a hammer and
nail to make the holes.*)
Piece of long string
Buttons

Fun and Games

GOOFY GOLF

Make an indoor golf game of skill for those stay-home afternoons.

You'll Need:

5 cleaned-out tin cans of different
   sizes
Paper clips
Construction paper
Wooden ice cream sticks
White glue
Markers
Small ball
Club (baseball bat, broom,
   golf club)

Here's How:

■ Put the cans in order from the largest to the smallest with the open ends facing out.

■ Cut out squares of paper and paste on the ends of wooden sticks. Glue the other end of each stick to a can.
■ Give the largest can the score of 2 and work up to 10 for the smallest one.
■ Clip the cans together tightly with paper clips.
■ Now practice putting with the ball and club. What is *your* best score?

Clank, clank!

Imagine it...North America throws out 40 billion pop cans in total each year. On average, that's about 150 cans per person. So, the next time you finish a pop, think before you throw. Is there another use for the can? Is there a recycling depot nearby? Who wants a world knee-deep in cans instead of grass and trees?

Here's How:

■ Thread the string through the holes.

■ Add a button on each end of the string before you tie a knot there.
■ Keep one can and give the other to a friend.
■ Pull the string taut and then whisper into the can to your friend.

Fantastic Faces

Make a fabulous face.
Will it be a frightening flashlight face?
Or a funny face sandwich to eat? Or both?

FLASHLIGHT FACES

Take an egg or some muffin ingredients, find a flashlight and make a spooky mask for Halloween.

You'll Need:

Egg Faces:
Egg white in a cup
Eggshell broken in tiny bits or strips of tissue
Hair drier
Flashlight
Glitter, make-up (optional)

Muffin Face:
Honey
Bran cereal
Corn meal
Water-based paints
Orange peel teeth
Flashlight

Here's How:

Egg Faces:

■ Smear the egg white on your face.
■ Stick the eggshell bits or tissue strips to it, and then smear more egg white over the shell bits or the ends of the strips.

■ Dry the egg white with the hair drier.
■ Hold a flashlight under your chin in a dark room and look in the mirror. **Yucko!**

Muffin Face:

■ Spread honey over your face, except around your eyes.
■ Stick the corn meal and bran to the honey.
■ Paint on eyebrows.
■ Pop in your orange peel teeth, and put a flashlight under your chin. **Aaaaaah!**

> **What is the longest word?**
>
> **Smiles (a mile between 2 S's)! And did you know that human beings are the only creatures in the world who smile when they're happy?**

FUNNY FACES

Invite your friends over to make their very own funny face sandwiches for lunch.

You'll Need:

Bread slices
Peanut butter or cheese spread
Eyes (radish slices, grape halves, cherry tomatoes, blueberries...)
Noses (carrot sticks, cucumber slices, cheese chunks...)
Smiles (avocado slices, apple eighths, orange pieces...)
Hair (bean sprouts, celery leaves, watercress leaves...)
Knives
Plates

Here's How:

■ Before your friends arrive, ask an adult to help you slice up the fruits and vegetables for face decorations.
■ Assemble the pieces on a platter.
■ Put out the bread and spreads.
■ Then let your friends start creating!

Fun and Games

Pick the Pairs

**Make some play clay markers
and have a game of "Pick the Pairs."**

You'll Need:

500 mL (2 cups) flour
125 mL (½ cup) salt
250 mL (1 cup) water
Mixing bowl, measuring cup,
   cookie tray
Rolling pin
Cutter (*A film tube or top of baby
   bottle or small jar works well.*)
Pencil
Poster paint, acrylic paint or
   magic markers
Paintbrushes
Clear nail polish

Here's How:

■ Mix the first three ingredients
together.
■ Roll out the play clay on a
smooth floured surface with a
rolling pin.

■ Make at least 30 round shapes
with the cutter. (A few extras may
be useful if you spoil any in the
next step.) They should be uniform
in size and appearance.
■ Create 15 pairs of markers by
making a different design on each
pair with a sharp pencil.
■ Let the markers sit on a cookie
tray overnight to dry.
■ The next day ask an adult to
heat the oven to 150°C (300°F).
Bake the markers for an hour.
■ After they have cooled, paint
them with bright colors.
■ For shiny markers, coat with
clear nail polish after paint is fully
dry.

**Kitchen
Challenge 5.**

**How can you give
away part of yourself,
but still keep it?**

**See page 66
for the answer.**

HOW TO PLAY

■ Place all the markers upside
down.
■ Turn them over two at a time
and look at the patterns. Do you
see a pair?
■ If yes, remove the pair from the
game. If no, turn the pieces upside
down and let a friend take a turn.
■ If you are playing by yourself,
try again. How long will it take
you to find all the pairs?

****If you are a checker fan,
paint nine markers black and
nine markers red.**

****If you like playing "Fish,"
double the recipe, and make
15 sets of markers, four with
the same pattern in each set.**

**Here are
some patterns
you might put
on your
markers.**

**What other
ones can you
think of?**

**Can you match up
the 11 pairs here?**

Fun and Games

Answers

Kitchen Challenge 1.

To see a chicken bone bend, place it in a glass of vinegar for a few days. The acid in the vinegar slowly eats away the hard calcium in the bone. A small leg bone takes about 5 days to go rubbery.

Kitchen Challenge 2.

All you have to do is roll the paper into a tube (about one thumb across) and tape! This makes the paper strong, rigid and round. The roundness ensures that the weight of the cookbook is evenly distributed when you place the book on top of the tube.

Kitchen Challenge 3.

When iodine is dropped on a food that contains starch, it turns black, and pretzels contain starch. Starch is a chain of simple sugars stored in plants, and it is one of the elements in food that gives you energy. What other foods in your kitchen contain starch? *WARNING: Do not eat any food tested with iodine; it is poisonous.*

Kitchen Challenge 4.

Place the ice cube in a dish of hot water and watch it flip—over and over and over!

Kitchen Challenge 5.

Use play clay and plaster of paris to make a foot or hand mold.

Here's How:

■ Make up a batch of the play clay recipe.

■ Pat out a pattie the size of your foot or hand to a depth of half a thumb.

■ Press your hand or foot into the play clay gently. Don't make a hole in the bottom!

■ Coat the indentation well with lots of cooking oil.

■ Mix up plaster of paris with water until it is the consistency of thick cream.

■ Pour this mixture into your body mold.

■ Let it sit overnight and then peel away the play clay. Be careful when peeling around the fingers.

■ Decorate, and give yourself away as a paperweight!

Party Fun

Come On Over!

Make some stamps to decorate your own party invitations and thank-you notes. While you're at it, design some great gift wrap and some placemats too. Ready? Set? Stamp!

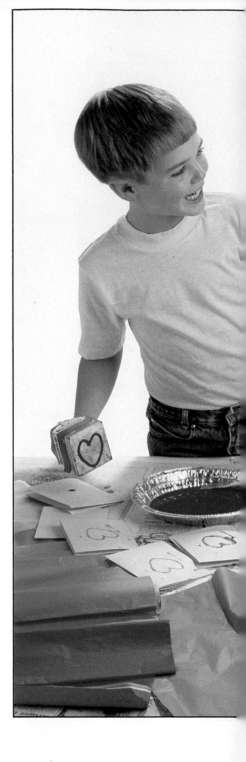

You'll Need:

Thick string
Scissors
White glue
Small milk cartons
Flat dishes or pans
Poster or powdered paint
Plain paper (*Typing or construction paper work well for cards. Grocery bags or tissue wrapping paper work well for gift wrap. Use thicker paper for placemats.*)
Newspaper

Here's How:

■ Using the white glue, draw a shape or write a word on the bottom of each milk carton.

■ REMEMBER: If you want to print a word, you'll have to write it backwards. To check your spelling, hold the stamp up to a mirror.

■ Cut a length of string long enough to fit the shape or word and press it down into the glue.

■ Let your stamps dry completely. This may take several hours.

■ Spread out newspaper on a flat surface.

■ Pour a thin layer of paint into a dish and fold the paper for your invitations. Line them up in a row on top of the newspaper.

■ Put your stamp into the paint and press down.

■ Lift the stamp up to see if all of the string has absorbed paint. When it has, let the excess paint drip off into the pan.

■ Do a few practice stamps on the newspaper before stamping the designs on your party invitations.

Getting Ready

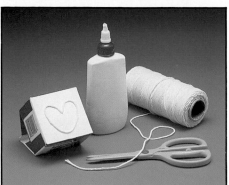

How much string do you have in your house?

Probably not as much as Francis Johnson of Minnesota. In 28 years he collected enough string to make a ball that weighed as much as two elephants and was as big as a small car!

No-Bake Cake

Here's a delicious cake that you "bake" in the freezer! Make it a day ahead of party time.

You'll Need:

24 chocolate chip cookies
175 mL (³/4 cup) uncooked oatmeal
125 mL (¹/2 cup) melted butter
2 L (¹/2 gallon) ice cream (*You can use two different flavors if you like.*)
1 plastic bag
Rolling pin
Bowl
Forks, spoons and a knife
24 cm (9¹/2 inch) springform pan
Decorations (*Try using grapes, berries, almonds, chocolate chips, colored sprinkles, smarties, jelly beans and other candies.*)

Here's How:

■ Put the ice cream in the fridge to soften slightly while you complete the following steps.
■ Put 16 cookies in a plastic bag and crush them well with the rolling pin.
■ Put the crushed cookies in a bowl and add 125 mL (¹/2 cup) oatmeal.
■ Add 75 mL (¹/4 cup) melted butter and stir.
■ Press this mixture evenly into the bottom of the pan.
■ Scoop out half the ice cream and smooth down on top of the crust with a metal spoon.
■ Now crush the rest of the cookies in the bag and mix with the remaining oatmeal and butter in a bowl.
■ Spread this mixture over the ice cream, and then add the rest of the ice cream to the pan.
■ Decorate the cake any way you like.
■ Freeze overnight. Before serving, run a knife around the edge of the pan and then remove the sides.
■ This cake serves about 12 people.

The biggest birthday party of all . . .

According to a Chinese tradition, *everybody's* birthday is celebrated on the Chinese New Year's Day along with the start of a new year.

Getting Ready

Hats On

Create high party spirits with these fabulous and funny hats. And who will hit the party piñata?

PARTY PIÑATA

Make this great game a couple of days ahead of time, and you'll be ready to celebrate the Latin American way.

You'll Need:

Large balloon (*Blow it up, tie the end and tape the end to a table.*)
Paste (*Mix 250 mL (1 cup) flour with 500 mL (2 cups) water in a bowl.*)
Newspaper sheets, cut into strips
Tape
Several long pieces of string
Decorating materials
Treats (wrapped candies, peanuts, raisin boxes . . .)
Blindfold
Baseball bat or stick

Here's How:

■ Spread a few newspaper sheets around the balloon to keep the table clean.
■ Dip the newspaper strips into the paste one by one.
■ Run your fingers down each strip to remove any extra paste.
■ Start wrapping the strips around the balloon, leaving an empty space at the neck about 8 cm (3 inches) in diameter.
■ First put on a layer of strips that go up and down.
■ Then put on a layer of strips that go around the balloon.

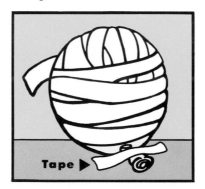

■ Let the piñata dry for three days and then pop the balloon.
■ Decorate the piñata and put the treats inside through the hole.
■ Now tape the ends of each piece of string inside the hole.

■ Reinforce each piece with tape several times, and then hang the piñata at eye level. Make sure there is lots of clear space around it.
■ When it's time to play the piñata game, give the first player a blindfold and the bat.
■ Make sure that everyone is standing well away from the player and the piñata, and then tell your friend to take three swings at the piñata. Then it is the next player's turn.
■ When the piñata breaks, everyone has a chance to scoop up the scattered treats.

SUPER HATS

Use this simple pattern and add odds and ends from around the house to make funny party hats.

You'll Need:

Newspaper sheets
Scissors
Glue or tape
Decorating materials (*Use cotton puffs, paper chains, material scraps and whatever else you can think of.*)

Getting Ready

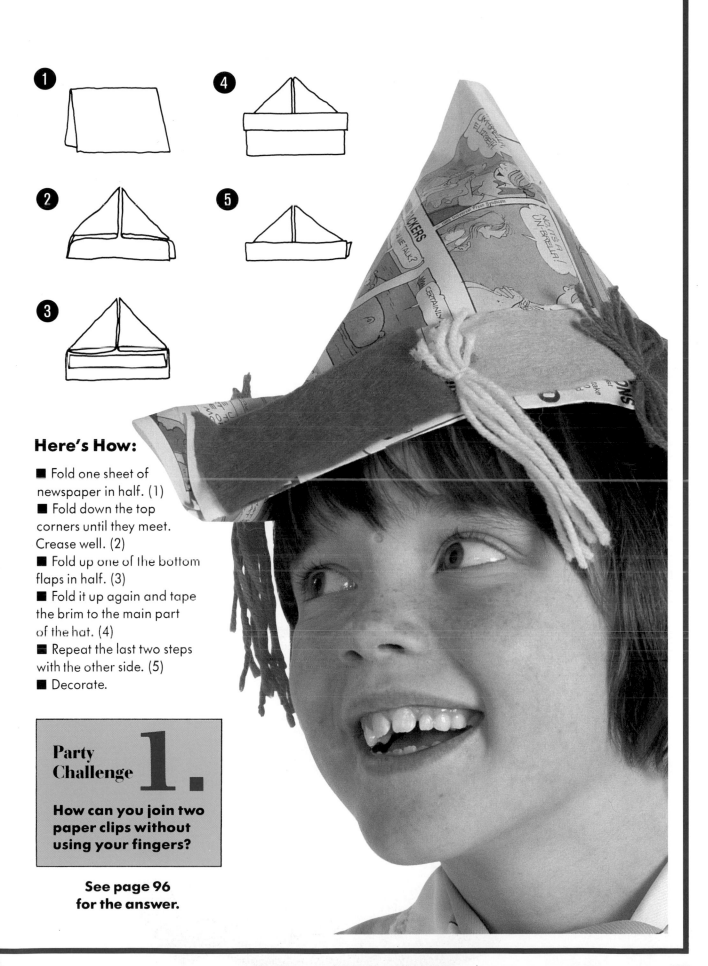

❶

❷

❸

❹

❺

Here's How:

■ Fold one sheet of newspaper in half. (1)

■ Fold down the top corners until they meet. Crease well. (2)

■ Fold up one of the bottom flaps in half. (3)

■ Fold it up again and tape the brim to the main part of the hat. (4)

■ Repeat the last two steps with the other side. (5)

■ Decorate.

Party Challenge 1.

How can you join two paper clips without using your fingers?

See page 96 for the answer.

Party Loot

Give your friends some tiny gifts to take home.
Everyone likes party loot!

DRESS-UP DISGUISE

Hook an egg-carton-cup nose onto a pair of toy glasses with pipe cleaners. Add a paper mustache if you like.

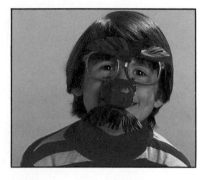

BATHTUB BOAT

Secure a toothpick mast in a styrofoam egg-carton cup or walnut half with plasticene. Poke on a sail made out of construction paper, and set sail for bathtubs unknown!

CREEPY CRAWLIES

Turn pebbles or stones into creepy-crawly creatures by decorating them with markers or paints. Tape on pipe cleaners for legs, feelers or wings.

Lucky Guests

A *potlatch* is a Northwest Coast Indian celebration often given to honor a person taking a new place in the village ranks. The word *potlatch* is a Chinook word meaning "to give." Today, children at a *potlatch* are given some money and candies, while grownups can receive blankets, towels, clothing and money. But long ago, shield-shaped sheets of beaten copper, blankets and even canoes were given away. Now that's a lot of loot!

LOOT BAGS

Make each guest a special loot bag to save their goodies in. If you like, your guests can decorate them when they arrive.

You'll Need:

Small paper bags
Scissors
White glue
Crayons or markers
Decorations (*Colored paper, tinfoil, pipe cleaners and cupcake liners all work well.*)

Here's How:

■ Fold over the top third of the paper bag.
■ Cut the corners off the folded flap and make a rounded nose.
■ Decorate the bag to look like any animal you want.

Getting Ready

74

Let's Decorate!

Add these great "surprise" decorations to the placemats created with your stamps, and your party will sparkle.

RIDDLE JARS

Decorate the party table with a riddle jar for each guest.

You'll Need:

Small clean jars (*Baby food jars work well.*)
Construction paper
White glue
Decorating materials (wool, sparkles, fabric scraps, paper cutouts)
Scissors
Colored markers and pencils
Treats
Riddles

Here's How:

■ Trace around the top of the jar twice on some paper.
■ Cut out each circle. Trim one circle so it fits snugly inside the lid.

■ On the bigger circle, print the riddle question. Print the answer on the smaller circle.
■ Glue the question circle to the top of the lid and then glue the answer circle to the inside. Let dry.
■ Decorate the jar, fill it with treats and put the lid on.
■ Repeat these steps until you have a jar for each guest.

BALLOON BUST

Burst balloons to discover where hidden treasure lies.

You'll Need:

Hiding places
Treats for all your guests
Paper and pencil
Scissors
Balloons
A few pins

Here's How:

■ Write a sentence describing where you have hidden the treats in your house. Leave plenty of space between the words.

Getting Ready

■ Cut the sentence up, leaving one word on each piece of paper.
■ Before you blow up each balloon, mark it with an X and then stuff one piece of paper into it.

■ When it's time to search for the hidden treasure, tell your guests to find and burst all the balloons marked with an X. (Don't hang them up too high!)
■ To find the treasure, they must put the words of the sentence in the proper order.

Party Challenge

2.

How can you make it impossible for a friend to lift up his or her ring finger?

See page 96 for the answer.

Giggle Games

How easily do you get the giggles? These party games are sure to get you started!

WHERE, OH WHERE, IS THE WONDERWART?

Pay attention, now. This is a very serious game . . . no laughing allowed!

You'll Need:

3 or more friends
Space large enough for your guests to sit in a circle

Here's How:

■ Tell your guests that when their turns come, they must turn to the person on their left and say, ''Friend, this is serious. Where, oh where, is the wonderwart?''
■ The whole group then places their right hands over their eyebrows, turns right, left and right again, saying ''Where, oh where, is the wonderwart?''

■ The person who has just been spoken to now turns to the person on his or her left, and so on.
■ The winner is the person who can keep a straight face the longest. No smirks, no smiles, no laughs allowed.

STARE DARE

Dare a friend to stare at you without laughing. Whoever laughs first is out, and another player steps up to challenge the winner.

Fun and Games

Feeling Low?

Put on a smile no matter how rotten you feel, and believe it or not, you may actually start to feel better. Some scientists believe that the movements your face muscles make when you smile send messages to your brain that make you feel happy. Try it!

ANIMAL NOISES

Ask your friends to sit in a circle while one blindfolded player stands in the middle. Give this player a long cardboard tube and spin him or her three times. The blindfolded player then gently taps someone in the circle. The person who has been tapped must make an animal noise. If the blindfolded player guesses who made the noise, they exchange places and the noisemaker is now "it." If not, spin the blindfolded player again and so on.

TONGUE TWISTERS

Who can say these phrases ten times fast?
- Toy boat
- Seven sleepy sheep
- Pink pig
- Rubber baby buggy bumpers

CHUCKLE BELLY

How long can you hold in the chuckles?

You'll Need:

Large area to spread out in Friends (the more, the merrier!)

Here's How:

- Ask one person to lie flat on his or her back.
- The second person puts his or her head on the first person's tummy.
- The other guests lie down in the same way, heads on each others' tummies, and wait for the chuckles to begin.

SWIMMING CHICKENS?

This is a crazy verison of "Simon Says." The leader calls out an animal action such as "Ducks fly!" Then he or she acts it out, and the guests follow suit. The leader calls out a second action, acts it out, and so on. BUT . . . once in a while the leader calls out a mixed-up animal action such as "Chickens swim!" Anyone who follows the leader and acts out the mix-up loses and must take over as leader.

Party Favorites

Try the memory game, pass the parcel and bounce a balloon . . . everyone will want to play!

PASS THE PARCEL

Who will find the small present inside the big package?

You'll Need:

Small prize
Small piece of gift wrap
Various containers ranging from
    small to large
Paper (plain brown paper,
    newspaper or gift wrap)
String
Tape
Scissors
Music

Here's How:

■ Wrap the prize in gift wrap.
■ Place the wrapped prize inside a bigger box and wrap it.
■ Continue wrapping in this manner until you have a large parcel to pass around a circle of guests.
■ Adding string can make the unwrapping tough . . . and fun!

■ The players sit in a circle. When the music starts, they pass the parcel from person to person. When the music stops, the player who has the parcel quickly starts to unwrap it. When the music starts again, the player must give up and pass it on.
■ The player who unwraps the prize can keep it!

Fun and Games

MEMORY TRAY

''Hmmmmmm . . . what was that skinny thing beside the apple? It was a . . . a . . . a shoelace. That's it!''
Play this game and find out how good *your* memory is.

You'll Need:

Tray
10-20 household objects
Pencils and paper (enough for your guests)
A watch

Here's How:

■ Before the party begins, arrange the objects on the tray. The older the guests, the more objects you can include.
■ Ask everyone to sit in a circle, and then put the tray in the middle.

■ Tell everyone they have one minute to look at the objects on the tray. Then they will be asked to write down (or draw, if they can't write) all the objects they can remember.
■ Keep an eye on your watch. When a minute is up, remove the tray and let your guests go to work. Whoever can remember the most objects wins the game.

Party Challenge 3.

How can you stick a pin into a balloon without bursting it?

See page 96 for the answer.

BALLOON BOUNCING

Set up a race course. Give each guest a blown-up balloon and tell them they must ''bounce'' the balloon across the finish line. Easy, right? Then tell them that they're not allowed to use their hands or let the balloon touch the ground!

Spider Web!

This spider game is great fun, even if you don't like spiders.

SEED SPIDERS

Turn pumpkin seeds into spiders and play "Stick the Spider on the Web."

You'll Need:

Clean, dry pumpkin seeds (*Use cardboard ovals if seeds are unavailable.*)

Markers or poster paints

Woolen legs (*Cut thumb-length pieces from different colored balls of wool. You'll need 4 short strands for each guest, plus some extras.*)

Yarn or string

Scissors

White glue

Web design on large piece of bristol board or cardboard

Masking tape

Blindfold

Here's How:

■ Before your guests arrive, create the bodies of the seed spiders.

■ Tie 4 legs together with a longer piece of yarn or string.

■ Glue the seed body and woolen legs together. Let dry.

■ Tape the spider-web design on a wall.

■ When the guests arrive invite them to decorate a spider for themselves.

■ Then stick a loop of masking tape on the bottom of each guest's spider.

■ Have each guest take 5 giant steps away from the web.

■ Blindfold the first player and spin him or her several times.

■ Then ask the player to "Stick the Spider on the Web!"

■ Whoever puts his or her spider closest to the center wins the game.

Fun and Games

Which is stronger, spider silk or steel?

Spider silk can be stronger than steel of the same thickness! It is also extremely versatile. Most spiders use it to spin webs. The amazing diving spider weaves a silken room underwater. Then it carries down bubbles of air to fill the room, and there it lives.

Handy Animals

Turn your hands into fabulous creatures by making these extraordinary hand puppets.

WOOLY PUPPETS

How many different creatures can you and your friends make?

You'll Need:

Old gloves or mittens (*Collect one for each guest.*)
Decorating materials (pipe cleaners, sparkles, construction paper . . .)
White glue in several dishes
Cotton swabs
Scissors

Here's How:

■ Put the decorating materials in the center of the table.
■ Lay a glove or mitten in front of each chair and invite your guests to sit down.
■ Give each guest a cotton swab to dip into the glue and let them start decorating.
■ When the puppets are finished, perform a party song!

Thumbs Up for Thumbs!

Thumbs are terrific! Without them, you'd find it difficult to do many things such as turning a door knob, or even holding this book. You don't believe it? Tape your thumbs to the sides of your hands and try living without them!

Fun and Games

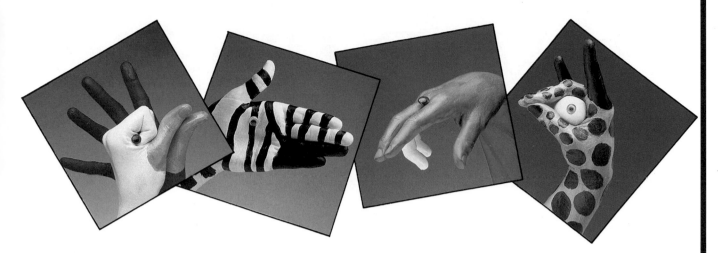

ANIMAL PUPPETS

Discover the animals waiting at your fingertips. All you need is some paint and imagination.

You'll Need:

Newspaper
Water-based poster paints
Baby oil
Paintbrushes
Dishes
Soap and water (to wash your
    hand afterwards)

Here's How:

■ Spread out newspaper on a large table and set up enough chairs for your guests.
■ Pour paint into the dishes and add a few drops of baby oil to each.
■ Then let your friends go wild with their paintbrushes!

V.I.P. Gifts

Grown-ups are V.I.P.s (Very Important People)...right?
Your parents, grandparents, aunts or uncles deserve the
very best, and what could be better than a picture of you?

BAKE A PHOTO

After you take these photos out of the oven and let them cool, they can be hung up.

You'll Need:

Photo frame dough (*Mix 575 mL (2¼ cups) flour, 250 mL (1 cup) salt and 250 mL (1 cup) water together in a bowl.*)
Rolling pin
Glass
2-8 photos, depending on size (*Small photos work best.*)
Fork
Straw
Cookie sheet
Paints or markers
Ribbon or wool
Oven preheated to 150°C (300°F)

Party Challenge 4.

How can you pick up an ice cube without using your fingers?

See page 96 for the answer.

Here's How:

■ Knead the dough. When it is smooth, roll it out on a well-floured surface until it's the consistency of thick pie crust.
■ Use the glass to cut out dough circles and place them on a cookie sheet.
■ After trimming the photos so that they are smaller than the circles, center each one on top of a dough circle.
■ Fold the dough edges over the photos and press them gently with a fork.
■ Poke a hole through the top of each photo frame with the straw.
■ Bake for an hour or until the dough is hard.
■ When the photo frames have cooled, decorate them and thread ribbons through the holes at the top.

Gifts to Make

PORTRAIT PAPERWEIGHT

Most V.I.P.s need help keeping their papers in order, so give them a paperweight.

You'll Need:

Photo of you (*A dried flower or a homemade picture also works well.*)
Clean, small jar with lid
Salt
Colored chalks
Metal strainer
Newspaper
White glue
Stir stick

Here's How:

■ Put the photo, face down, in the bottom of the jar.
■ Pour a handful of salt onto a folded piece of newspaper. (1)
■ Hold the strainer over the salt. Now rub the chalk through the mesh and onto the salt. (2)
■ Stir the chalk and salt together until evenly mixed.
■ Now use the newspaper to pour part of the mixture into the jar.
■ Start again, but this time, use a different color of chalk or plain salt, so you can build up pretty layers in the jar. (3)

■ When the jar is full, gently shake it to remove any air pockets and add a little more salt.
■ Line the inside edge of the lid with white glue. (4)
■ Tightly screw the lid in place and turn the jar over. Now your face beams out from on top!

H.C. STORM SCHOOL

Easy Pizazz

These little extras are easy to make, and fun to give any time. Jazz up a special friend!

JAZZY JEWELRY

String some paper beads and make a hit!

You'll Need:

Old color magazines
(Ask an adult if you can cut them up.)
Pencil
Scissors
White glue
Yarn
Safety pin

Here's How:

■ Cut long triangles out of the magazine pages. The base of each triangle should measure about 5 cm (2 inches). (1)

■ Squeeze a line of white glue down one side of the triangle. (2)

■ Start at the wide end of the triangle and roll it tightly around a pencil. (3)

■ When the glue is dry, pull the pencil out.

■ String the beads on yarn end-to-end to make a bracelet or necklace. (4)

■ For an ''Egyptian'' effect, ask an adult to use a needle and thread to string the beads side-by-side. To make a brooch, ask an adult to push a safety pin through the back of a bead.

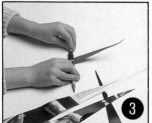

Gifts to Make

FANCY LACES

Decorate plain, white shoelaces with colored markers, and your friends can have the fanciest feet on the block. Don't forget to make some for yourself!

NOODLE NECKLACE

To make a nifty necklace, collect pasta pieces of all shapes and sizes. Color them with markers and string them on brightly colored yarn.

Living Jewelry

Believe it or not, thousands of years ago Greek women made musical barrettes by stringing cicada bugs in their hair on golden threads.

Super Stuffers

Quarters and dimes,
Scissors and string!
Where can you put
All of these things?
Inside these two easy-to-make containers, of course!

OINK BANK

Turn a plain, old bleach bottle into a piggy bank with class.

You'll Need:

Clean bleach bottle with cap
Corks or empty spools
Construction paper
Felt
Pipe cleaners
Scissors
White glue

Here's How:

■ Lay the bottle on its side and ask an adult to help you cut a slit big enough for coins to fit through.
■ On the opposite side, cut two holes big enough for the cork or spools to slide into for feet. Be sure the holes are set far enough apart to let the bank stand upright.

■ Use the cap as the pig's nose, and use the paper, felt and pipe cleaners to make ears, eyes and a tail.
■ Oink, Oink!

PATCHWORK PENCIL HOLDERS

Collect some empty cans and fabric scraps. Then start patching!

You'll Need:

Empty cans
Fabric scraps
White paper
Tape
Scissors
White glue

Here's How:

■ Cover each can with a piece of white paper. Tape to secure.
■ Cut the fabric into squares, circles or any shapes you like.
■ Glue the scraps onto the cans to make a patchwork design.

Is a pig a pig?

No, it isn't. Unlike other animals such as dogs and cats, a pig will not overeat. It knows exactly when it's had enough and stops before it's stuffed!

Gifts to Make

Just for the Fun of It!

Here are some games to make and give away. But they're so much fun, you may want to keep them yourself.

TWO-IN-ONE GAME

Turn one cardboard box into two great games. Then try out your tossing skills!

You'll Need:

Large cardboard box
Scissors
Rolled-up pair of old socks
Paint

Markers
Clothespegs or ice cream sticks
3 rings (*Cut rings from yogurt
  container lids or use rubber
  canning rings.*)
Paper and pencil

Gifts to Make

Here's How:

■ On one side of the box paint a face, and after it has dried, cut out a big, wide mouth.

■ On the other side, paint 9 widely-spaced dots and number them. Poke clothespegs or ice cream sticks through each dot.

■ Put the rings into the box along with the socks.

■ Write out these instructions on a card:

Sock Toss: Can you toss the socks through the mouth? Each time you do, take a step backward. How far can you step back and still throw the socks into the mouth?

Ring Toss: Stand back and toss the rings at the clothespegs or ice cream sticks. When a ring lands on a peg, add the number of the peg to your score.

CHALLENGE CUP

How long will it take to get a "cup in one?"

You'll Need:

Ruler
38 cm (15 inches) of string
Paper drinking cup (*Decorate to make the gift extra special.*)
Tape
Paper and pencil

Here's How:

■ Turn the cup upside down and poke a small hole through the bottom.

■ Thread the string through the hole and knot securely.

■ Tie the other end of the string to the end of the ruler and tape in place.

■ Write out these instructions on a card:

Hold the ruler in one hand. How many times in a row can you get the cup to land on top of the ruler?

Party Challenge 5.

How can you turn yourself into a mindreader?

See page 96 for the answer.

Pet Presents

If you and your friends love pets, share some party fun with them too!

KITTEN CRAZES

Give your kitten a set of balls made out of crumpled newspaper or construction paper. To make the balls especially appealing, rub catnip on them! Kittens love to chase these paper balls. They also love to pounce on rope "snakes." To make a snake, simply cut off a *thick* piece of nylon twine. (Avoid using long pieces of string, thread or elastic for this game.)

HAMSTER HIDEAWAYS

Make some hideaway tunnels for your hamster out of empty cardboard tubes. Decorate them with non-toxic markers and place them in the hamster cage. Hamsters like hiding in them … they may even sleep in them and chew on them too!

Which pets have been around the longest?

Dogs were probably the first wild animals to become tame pets. Their ancestors, wolflike animals, came close to campfires for tidbits, and eventually people kept the friendliest ones around permanently. While dogs have lived around people as long as 12,000 years, cats have been around for about 4,000 years, and goldfish have been bred for over 1,000. That's some history!

DOGGONE DOG BONES

Your hound will gobble these snacks up lickety-split.

You'll Need:

375 mL (1½ cup) whole wheat flour, 125 mL (½ cup) grated cheese, 50 mL (¼ cup) bacon fat, 125 mL (½ cup) water and 15 mL (1 tbsp) soya sauce (*Mix together well.*)
Greased cookie sheet
Bowl
Fork
Oven preheated to 200° C (400° F)

Here's How:

■ Mould small pieces of dough into bone shapes. The "bones" should be no more than 1 cm (½ inch) thick.
■ Place on the cookie sheet.
■ Bake for 30 minutes.
■ When cool, store in a paper bag.

Gifts to Make

WARNING:
Don't give these
biscuits to dogs
with heart disease
or those on
low-sodium diets.
The biscuits are
high in salt.

Answers

Party Challenge 1.

Fold one long strip of paper into thirds as shown below. Join the first two sections with a paper clip, then the second two sections with another paper clip. Stand well away from other people and pull hard on both ends of the paper. Ta da!

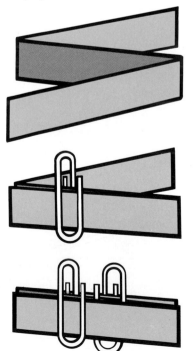

Party Challenge 2.

Ask a friend to place his or her hand on a table, palm down with fingers spread out. Now ask your friend to tuck the middle finger under. Can he or she lift the ring finger?

Party Challenge 3.

Blow up a balloon three-quarters full and knot it. Make a cross out of clear tape on the balloon. Now push a straight pin through the center of the tape cross! WARNING: Hold onto the balloon and pin tightly, and be sure to pull out the pin before putting the balloon down.

Party Challenge 4.

All you need in addition to the ice cube is some salt and a piece of string. Lay the end of a wet piece of string on top of the ice cube. Sprinkle some salt on top and wait about one minute. Then lift.

Party Challenge 5.

You need to plan this "mind-reading" trick with a friend in advance. You leave the room while your friend and the others stay in the room and decide upon an object. When you return, you have to guess what the object is. You do not speak. (You're too busy "concentrating" on the image in everyone's minds!) Your friend asks you if various objects in the room are the right ones. The question about the correct item always comes after your friend asks about a *black* object.

Outdoor Fun

Build a Scarecrow

Here's a garden scarecrow that the birds will want to stay away from!

You'll Need:

2 wooden stakes (one about half the length of the other)
Rope
Decorated head (bucket, stuffed pillowcase, old soccer ball . . .)
Old brightly colored scarves
Pie-plate necklace (*String several tinfoil pie plates together.*)
Clothes that billow in the wind
String
Nails

Here's How:

■ Make a body frame by attaching the smaller stake about one third of the way down the longer stake. Loop rope around the place where the two stakes meet until secure, then knot.
■ Secure the head to the top of the long stake. (*Tie the pillowcase on with rope, or slit the soccer ball and push onto the stake*.)
■ Birds are scared away by sudden motion, so dress your scarecrow in billowy clothes. Don't forget the scarves!

■ Birds dislike unexpected noises, so add a pie-plate necklace to clatter in the wind.
■ Birds avoid strings or nets that get in the way of flying, so give your scarecrow long string fingers that reach down to the ground. Tie nails to the end of each string and anchor the fingers by pushing the nails into the ground.
■ Your scarecrow is ready to go to work. Try to move him every once in a while so the birds don't get used to him.

Outdoor Challenge 1.

How can you transform a small rectangular piece of paper into a mini-helicopter?

See page 126 for the answer.

Catch the Wind

Twister Kite

Make this kite out of garbage bags and sticks, and send it flying high!

You'll Need:

2 crosspiece sticks, each 14 inches long (*Wooden dowels from your hardware store work well.*)

1 stick, 18 inches long (*This will be the spine of your kite.*)

2–3 large colored plastic garbage bags, or try decorating your own! (*Cut down each side so they all open up into long strips. Tape together end to end.*)

Scissors
Masking tape
Crayons or pen
Kite string
Bridle (*Measure out 24 inches of string and tie a loop near the middle.*)
Big safety pin
A strong breeze

What is a Thai Snake?
It's the largest kite ever flown. Incredibly, it's nearly as long as six football fields!

Here's How:

■ Tape each crosspiece about 4 inches from each end of the spine stick. Then tie securely with string. (1)

■ Make a string frame around the outside of the crosspieces as shown. Loop the string around the sticks many times and tape so it does not slip. (1)

■ Put the kite frame at the top of the garbage-bag strip. Trace around the frame. Add a 1-inch border around the top and sides of the tracing. Cut out along this border. (2)

■ Remove the frame, turn the strip over, and fold the plastic in half. Draw the tail as shown and cut out. (3)

■ Attach the head to the frame by taping the border edges over the string. Tape well.

■ Turn the kite over. Punch two small holes just above each crosspiece. (4)

■ Thread the bridle string through these holes. After tying a knot to secure each end, tape the holes well. (4)
READY, SET, FLY!

■ Attach the safety pin to the end of your flying line.

■ Use the safety pin to attach the flying line to the loop in the bridle, and you're all set! (4)

■ Hint: If your kite twists too much, add more tail. If you can't launch the kite, cut some of the tail off.

■ **WARNING:** *Fly your kite in an open space. Never fly it near power lines.*

Catch the Wind

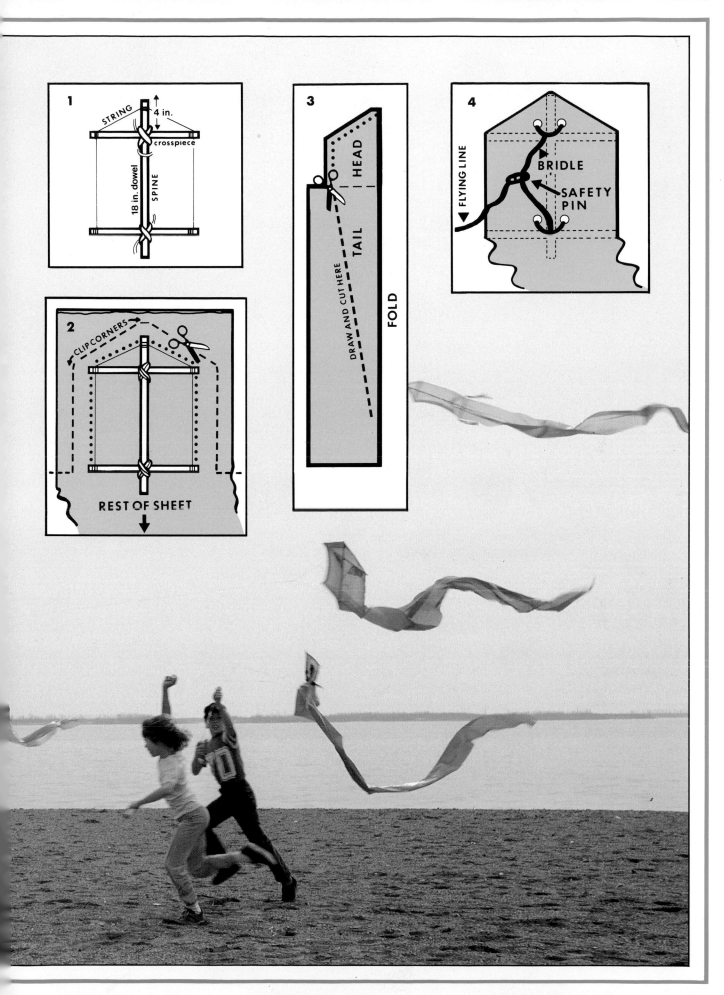

1
STRING
4 in.
crosspiece
18 in. dowel
SPINE

2
CLIP CORNERS
REST OF SHEET

3
HEAD
TAIL
DRAW AND CUT HERE
FOLD

4
FLYING LINE
BRIDLE
SAFETY PIN

Windchimes

Catch the wind and let it make music for you. Hang these chimes in a tree or on a balcony – anywhere the wind blows freely.

You'll Need:

Old keys that nobody needs (*Your local locksmith may have extra ones to give you.*)
10 feet of ribbon or yarn
Mason jar lid or coat hanger
Scissors

Here's How:

☐ Cut 5-10 equal lengths of ribbon or yarn.
☐ Tie the keys to the ribbon or yarn pieces.
☐ Tie the top ends of the pieces to the mason jar lid or coat hanger.
☐ Hang your chimes in a breezy spot and wait for the wind!

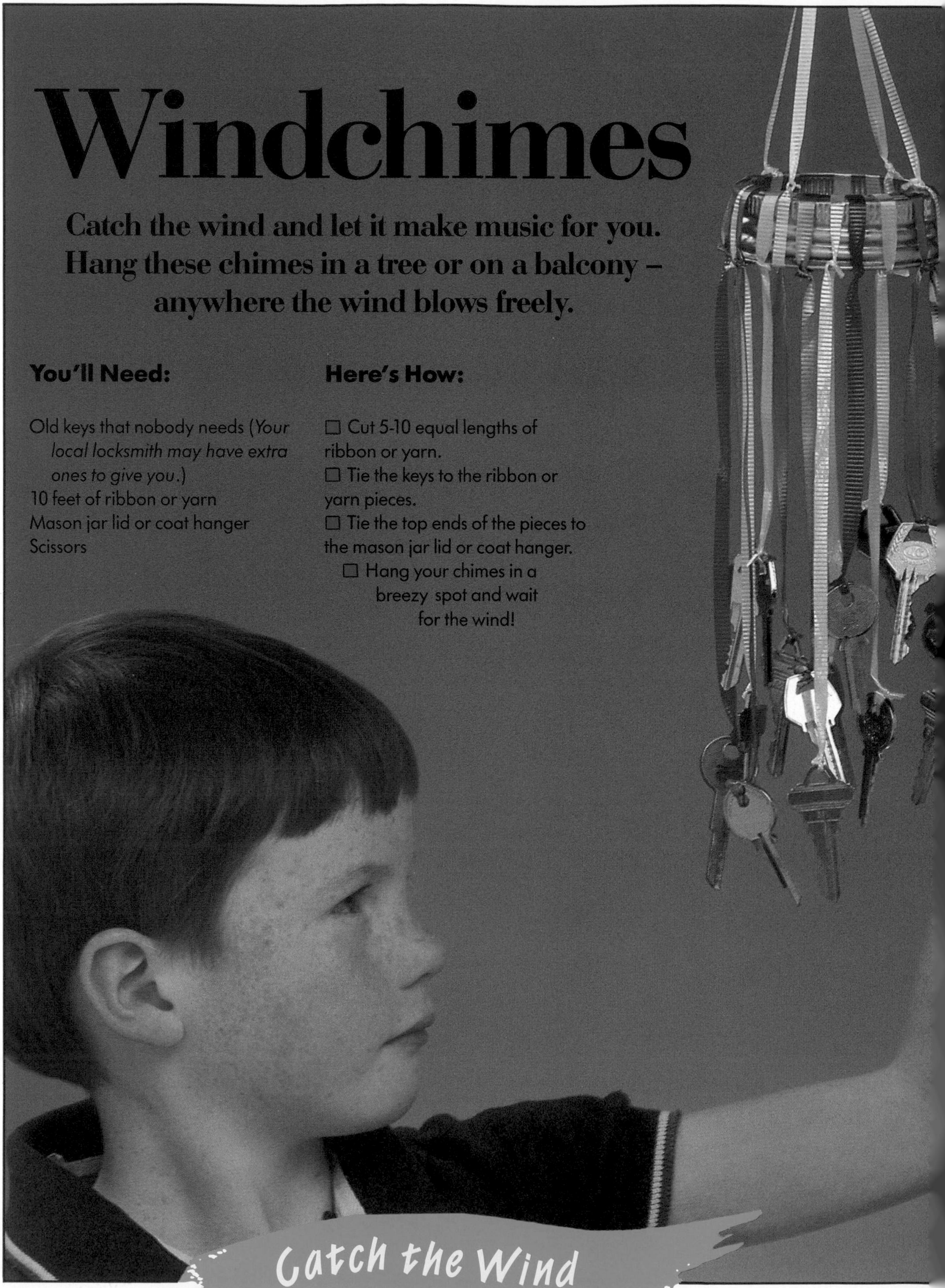

Catch the Wind

A Windy Day Fact

Did you ever wonder why you feel cooler when the wind is blowing? Hot food cools down more quickly when you blow on it. In the same way, the wind carries your body heat away faster than still air, making you feel colder.

Juggling

Juggling takes some practice, but once you get those balls rolling you'll amaze your friends and family.

You'll Need:

2 or 3 knotted scarves (*Start with these before trying balls or fruit.*)

2 or 3 different colored tennis balls (slit and filled with about 50 pennies) or a couple of apples or oranges

Here's How:

■ Go outside and give yourself lots of room to practice.

■ Stand with your feet apart, your arms bent at the elbow and your palms facing up.

■ Imagine two Xs directly above your hands at eye level. When you juggle, keep your eyes on the Xs, not your hands. (1)

■ Try throwing one ball straight up, using only your lower arm and keeping your wrist stiff. Practice with each hand. (2)

■ Now toss a ball with your right hand to the X opposite your left eye. Catch the ball with your left hand. (3)

■ Pop it back the other way. Practice popping one ball back and forth until you can do it smoothly. (3)

■ Now try two balls! Hold one ball in each hand. Pop the first ball up to the opposite X spot. When the ball reaches that spot, pop the second ball to the other X spot. Practice! (4)

■ Now try three balls. Hold two balls in one hand and one in the other. Start popping the balls as with just two balls, but before you catch the second ball, pop the third. (5)

Fun and Games

Let's have a big hand for these talented hands!

One famous performer, Enrico Rastelli, can actually juggle an amazing 10 balls at once. Some professional entertainers also juggle knives, plates and flaming torches. Real masters can juggle blindfolded, on a trapeze or on a unicycle. Wow!

Backyard Olympics

These games are fun – and a challenge! Test your skills. Which ones can you do?

EGG AND SPOON RACE

And they're off! Who will keep the egg in the spoon?

You'll Need:

1 or more friends
Several tablespoons
Eggs or Ping-Pong balls

Here's How:

■ Mark a starting line and a finish line on the ground.
■ For a real challenge, add some obstacles — boxes to step over, chairs to go under, trees to go around . . . .
■ Give each friend a spoon with an egg or ball in it.
■ On your mark, get set, go!
■ Whoever reaches the finish line first without dropping the egg or ball wins!

Fun and Games

JUICE CAN RACE

Who will be first across the finish line?

You'll Need:

1 or more friends
2 large empty juice cans for each friend (*Use cans that have been opened with a punch-type opener.*)

Here's How:

■ Ask your friends to wear sneakers so that they don't slip.
■ Mark a starting line and finish line on the ground.
■ You all must use the cans as stepping stones. While you're standing on one can, you must move the second can in front of you and then step onto it. Move the other can, step and so on.
■ No part of your body may touch the ground or you must go back to the beginning and start all over again!

PAPER PLATE PITCH

Ready? Aim. Pitch . . . and try again!

You'll Need:

Empty box or barrel
Stack of paper plates

Here's How:

■ Mark a line on the ground.
■ Set the box about 2 body lengths in front of the line.
■ How many paper plates can you toss into the box?

LEMON WALK

Don't put that lemon in the fridge. Put it . . . between your *knees*?

You'll Need:

3 or more friends (divided into 2 teams)
2 lemons
2 large empty plastic containers

Here's How:

■ Set up the containers 2 body lengths in front of each team.
■ The first player on each team puts a lemon between his or her knees, runs to the container and drops the lemon in.

■ The player picks up the lemon, runs back to the start and gives it to the next player. (This is the only time you can touch the lemon with your hands.)
■ If the player drops the lemon or tips the container over, he or she must return to the starting line and begin again.
■ The first team to finish wins the lemon walk.

Outdoor Challenge 2.

How can you make it impossible for someone to lift up his or her foot?

See page 126 for the answer.

Warm Up!

These Inuit games are fun to play and great for building up your muscles.

NAUKTAK

''Sam's Jumping Game'' is good for developing strength in your lower body.

■ Lie down and put your feet flat against a wall.

■ Put a pencil on the floor to mark where your head is.

■ Now get up and crouch with your back to the wall. Can you leap as far as the pencil?

The games you see here are hundreds of years old.

These games were part of every Inuit child's survival training. Without strong muscles and quick reflexes for hunting, fishing and guiding dog sleds, they wouldn't survive long in one of the harshest climates in the world — the Arctic winter. Today only some Inuit kids live in the traditional way of their ancestors, but most still play these games for fun.

TU NU MIU

''The Backpush'' develops strength in your trunk, legs and lower body.

■ Find a friend and mark a line on the ground.

■ Sit back to back so the line is in between you.

■ Can you push yourself over the line first?

■ No cheating! You can use your hands and feet only for balance and leverage!

On the Move

TILIRAGINIK QIRIQTAGTUT

This "Jump Through Stick" exercise develops your flexibility.

■ Hold a stick in front of you. Your hands should be about a shoulder width apart.

■ Jump over the stick without letting go and land on both feet.

■ Now try jumping backward.

■ How many times can you do it without stopping?

Don't overdo these exercises. Build your strength up gradually. If you have back or neck problems, ask your doctor first.

H.C. STORM SCHOOL

Hiking Gear

Thinking about a city or country safari? Then take along this special equipment and be ready for adventure.

JUICE JUG

Make a portable cooler to keep your juice fresh and cool.

You'll Need:

Medium-sized milk carton
Insulation (*Styrofoam bits or shredded newspaper*)
Scissors
Chilled can or box of juice
Fastener (paper clip, clothespin . . .)
Decorating materials (optional)

Here's How:

■ Open up the milk carton carefully and clean it out.
■ Put a thick layer of insulation in the bottom and place the can or box of juice on top.
■ Stuff the rest of the insulation around the juice.
■ Close the spout of the milk carton tightly with a fastener.
■ If you like, decorate the cooler.

BUDDY SCOPE

"Look at that bird!"
"Where?"
"There!"
"Where? I still can't see it."
Now you can see what your friend sees — with a great buddy scope.

You'll Need:

2 empty paper towel tubes of
    equal size
Masking tape
Cardboard rectangle (as long
    as the tubes and about
    1 foot wide)

Here's How:

■ Tape the tubes onto the same side of the cardboard, parallel to each other.
■ One tube should be on the far left side, the other on the far right.
■ When you spot something interesting on your hike, look through the scope with your friend. Now you can both see it at once.

Imagine hiking around the world!

It took Steven Newman 4 years, 40 million steps, and only 4 pairs of shoes. He finished his world trek in April 1987.

On the Move

Super Sandals

Save comic and color sections from the newspaper to make fun summer sandals for you and your friends.

You'll Need:

About 20 newspaper sheets folded into strips about a thumb-length wide
Clear tape
White glue
Scissors
Crayon or pencil

Here's How:

■ Wind 1 strip tightly into a narrow oval shape. (1)
■ Tape the next strip to the loose end of your oval. Wind this new strip around the oval. (1)

■ Continue winding and taping until the oval is nearly as large as your foot.
■ Strengthen the sandal by winding a strip around the width of the oval. Tape in place. (2)

On the Move

■ Now continue winding strips of paper tightly around the oval until it is as long as your foot. Glue and tape the end securely. (3)

■ Repeat for the second sandal.

■ Trace the finished soles. Then place each tracing over 1 sheet of colored newspaper. Cut out the traced patterns. (4)

■ Paste 1 cutout to the top of each sandal.

■ Turn the sandal over. Take the end of a long folded strip and push it in between two folds in the sole. Turn the sandal right side up and bring the other end of the strip up and over the sandal and down to the other side of the sole. Be sure to leave enough room for your foot before tucking the other end of the strip in. Secure the strips with glue and tape. Paint each sandal with thin layer of glue, top and bottom.

■ Dry well before wearing.

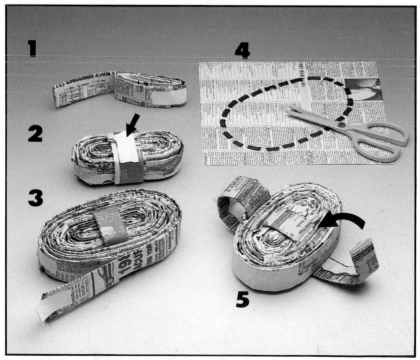

On Parade

Give yourself some good luck! Make a wonderful Chinese dragon with your friends and family and go on parade.

You'll Need:

Old, single-sized sheet (folded in half)
Scissors
Big nail or one-hole punch
Masking tape
Newspaper
Paint and brushes
Ball of yarn
Large box
White glue
Paper cups, egg cartons, tennis balls
Shiny decorations
Twist ties or pipe cleaners
4–5 hula hoops. Or take some old wire coat hangers and form them into hoops. Wrap masking tape around the place where the two ends meet. (Ask an adult to help you!)

Outdoor Challenge 3.

This book was written in the Year of the Dragon! Which animal year were you born in?

Turn to page 126 for the answer.

Here's How:

1. MAKE THE BODY:

■ Ask an adult to help you cut the sheet as shown in the diagram. (1)
■ Now use a nail or punch to punch holes around the sheet as shown here. Reinforce the holes with masking tape.
■ Paint the sheet and thread yarn through the holes along the bottom — the more colorful the better!

2. MAKE THE HEAD:

■ Cut a big hole in the bottom of the box for the mouth. Make sure you can see through it. (2)
■ Cut two smaller holes on top for the dragon's horns. (2)
■ Push rolled newspaper cones up through these holes and glue in place.
■ Paint and decorate the head with egg carton nostrils, tennis ball eyes, ribbon, tinsel or whatever else you can think of.

3. PUT THE HEAD AND BODY TOGETHER:

■ Overlap the front end of the sheet over the back end of the box.
■ Punch holes in the box to match those in the sheet.
■ Join the sheet and box together by looping twist ties or pipe cleaners through each set of holes. (3)
■ Attach hoops to the rest of the sheet with twist ties wherever there are two sets of holes.

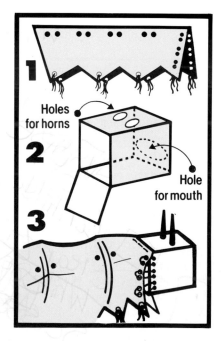

Holes for horns

Hole for mouth

On the Move

Satellite

Shooting Stars

ORION

3.

1.

2.

4.

Stargazing

The next time you stay up late, look up . . . look way up and spot some of these sights in the night sky. Which one will you see first? Remember that the farther you go away from bright city lights, the more stars you'll see.

Starry Nights

THE MILKY WAY

This huge spiral-shaped group of 100,000 million stars is the galaxy Earth belongs to. It looks like a misty glowing band of stars stretching across the night sky.

CAN YOU FIND ORION, THE HUNTER?

Orion is one of the constellations, or star groups, that have been mapped by astronomers. If you go stargazing between January and April, Orion is easy to see.

■ If you are north of the equator, look south for Orion. If you are south of the equator, look north for an upside-down Orion.
■ While you're looking at Orion, see if you can spot a faint fuzzy patch near his belt. This is a nebula, one of the many clouds of gas in the universe from which new stars are created.
■ Can you find Betelgeuse, an old star or ''red giant,'' on Orion's shoulder? The redder a star is, the older and cooler it is. Also, try spotting young Rigel, a bluish-white star, on Orion's right foot.

ORION	
1. Orion's Belt	**3.** Betelgeuse
2. Nebula	**4.** Rigel

SHOOTING STARS

Shooting stars are not stars at all. They are meteors: small pieces of rock or dust from outer space. When one of these pieces falls through Earth's atmosphere, it burns white hot and shines briefly. Perhaps you'll spot a fireball, a really bright meteor!

Star or Satellite?

Any slow, steadily moving white point of light is not a star at all, but a satellite! (A plane flashes colored lights.)

Flying Saucers

**Is it a bird? Is it a plane?
No, it's a U.F.O. — handmade by you!
The next time the moon is full,
turn some paper plates into flying saucers
and have a game of catch by moonlight.**

You'll Need:

Paper dinner plates or tinfoil pie
    plates
Plastic yogurt container (optional)
Play clay (*Mix together 1 1/4 cups
    flour, 1/4 cup salt and 1/2 cup
    water in a bowl with your
    fingers.*)
Tinfoil
Scissors
Tape (*Clear tape looks the best.*)
Bright shiny decorations and paint
    (*Reflector tape, tinfoil and non-
    toxic ''glow in the dark'' paint
    and/or fluorescent paint are
    especially effective.*)
Glue
Paintbrush

Here's How:

■ Turn a plate upside down.
■ Roll out a play clay ''snake''
long enough to fit around the rim
of the plate.
■ Roll the snake on to the tinfoil
and then wrap the foil around the
snake. Set aside.
■ Paint and decorate the plate
with as much shiny stuff as you
can find.
■ When done, securely tape the
snake on to the rim of the plate.
■ Choose a night when the moon
is full and ask your parents if you
may play outside. Then find some
friends and shoot your U.F.O.
around the yard or park. Be sure
to play on a clear stretch of land
where there are no objects hidden
in the shadows to stumble over.

Starry Nights

■ Try out two variations on the basic design and see which one flies best. (1) Cut out a circle in the center of the plate or (2) Add a plastic container to your saucer. (Trace the small end of the container in the middle of the plate and cut out this circle. Now make tiny cuts around the edge of the hole. Push the upside-down plate halfway down the container until snug and tape firmly in place.)

Outdoor Challenge 4.

How can you tell if the moon is getting bigger or smaller?

See page 126 for the answer.

Super-duper Dog Wash

Follow these tips and become the best dog washer on the block.

You'll Need:

Warm, sunny day
Brush
Tub
Big plastic container or scoop
Shampoo (*Non-perfumed baby shampoo or dog shampoo works best.*)
Garden hose
Towels
Hair drier (optional)

Here's How:

■ Ask a friend over. It always helps to have an extra pair of hands!

■ Take your dog and a tub of lukewarm water outside.

■ Brush your dog first to remove loose hair and dirt.

■ Ask your dog to stand in the tub of water. Praise your dog, who might be nervous, all through the bath.

■ Use the scoop to gently soak the fur with water from the tub.

■ Massage shampoo into the coat until lathery. Be careful not to get any shampoo in your dog's eyes.

■ Turn the water on low volume. Rinse your dog by holding the nozzle of the hose close to the fur.

■ Spend three times as long on the rinse as the shampoo. Any shampoo left behind can cause an itchy rash or dandruff.

■ Towel your dog down, move him or her to a dry area and let your dog sniff the hair drier.

■ Use the drier on a cool setting to blow the fur in the opposite direction.

■ **WARNING: *Do not use the drier near any water.***

■ If your dog doesn't like the drier, play with him or her while brushing the fur until dry.

> ### A sidewalk is like a giant nail file . . .
> **To a dog, that is! It keeps a dog's nails short and trim.**

Waterworks

Cool Off!

The next time you're sweltering in the heat, put on a swimsuit and try these watery cool activities.

GIANT BUBBLES

Blow the biggest bubbles on the block!

You'll Need:

3 tbsp. glycerine (from your drugstore)

1 cup dishwashing detergent

12 cups water

Large tub (*A baby's plastic swimming pool or a big laundry tub works well . . . the larger the better!*)

Sturdy giant circular blower (large plastic ring, small hula hoop, or 8 or more big plastic straws threaded with heavy string. Or ask an adult to bend a coat-hanger wire into a circle, then cover it with plastic straws)

Here's How:

■ Go outside. Mix the water, glycerine and detergent in the tub.
■ Hold the sides of your blower and lay it flat in the water.
■ Lift it out slowly.
■ Hold your blower into the wind and watch your giant bubble fly.

GLOVE SPRINKLER

Have some wild, wet fun with a hose and an old rubber glove.

Cut off the fingertips of the glove. Attach the wrist of the glove securely to the hose with several elastic bands and some string. Turn on the water and look out!

ICE CAPADES

Invite your friends over for an outdoor afternoon of ice sculpting.

Freeze water or a mixture of juice and water in empty milk cartons or plastic containers two nights before. When your friends arrive, give them garbage bag aprons and challenge them to create something great out of the ice blocks . . . using only their mouths and fingers!

A Giant Ice Cube?

Scientists are exploring the idea of towing icebergs by ship to hot, dry parts of the world in need of fresh water. That's quite a challenge. Some icebergs are as big as the country of Belgium and tower as high as an office building!

Waterworks

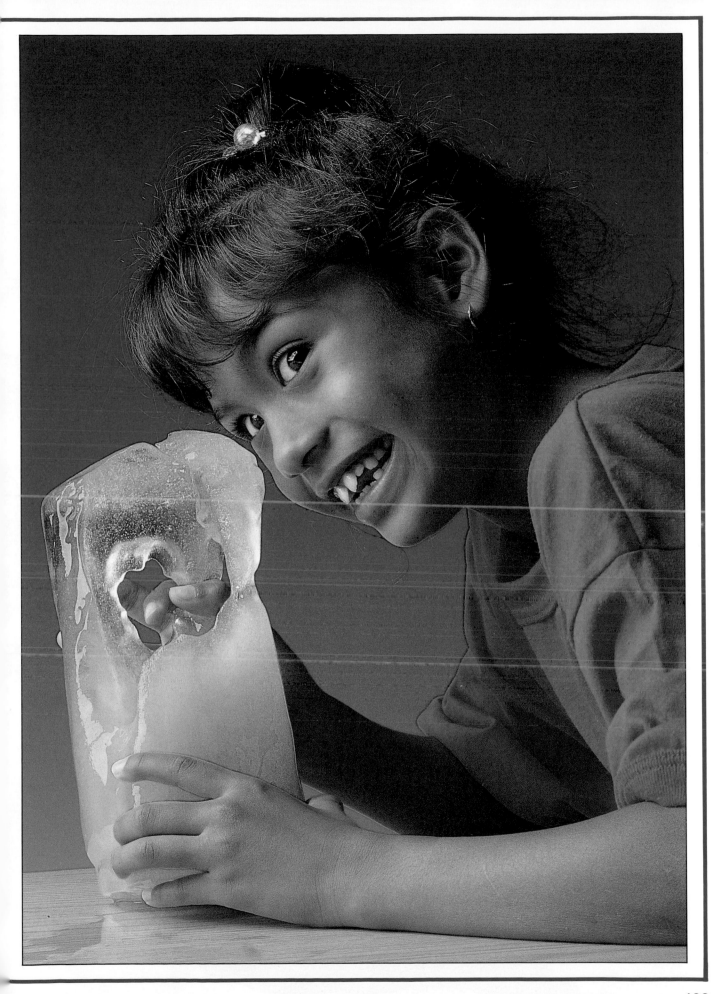

Something's Fishy...

Can you spot why the fish in this river are in trouble? Follow the numbers on the picture and read the related clues. Which ones are trouble spots? Which things help the fish?

1. Water temperature is 55°F.

2. Kids remove garbage from stream.

3. Farmer sprays orchard with pesticide.

4. Oil spills into river.

5. Overhanging bushes attract insects.

6. Cattle are in the river.

7. A tree has fallen into the river.

8. River runs through city park.

9. Garbage dump leaks into lake.

10. There are lots of small fish to eat.

11. Sewage pipe empties into lake.

12. Pipe sucks water into power station.

Waterworks

8.

2.

9.

KEEP OUT

10.

11.

7.

6.

12.

5.

SAN MURATA

Answers continued
on page 126.

Outdoor Challenge 5.

Take a look around your neighborhood. What things could you do to help the environment?

ANSWERS: 1. The given temperature is just right. Fish eggs and young fish can be seriously harmed if the stream gets too hot or cold. **2.** Removing garbage makes the stream a cleaner place. **3.** Even small amounts of chemicals can be deadly to fish. **4.** Fish can't breathe well in oily water. **5.** Overhanging bushes attract bugs for fish to eat. **6.** Cattle stir up the stream bottom and pollute the water. **7.** The river swishes around the tree, taking earth and mud from under it. Deep pools are formed in which the fish can rest or hide.

Answers

Outdoor Challenge 1.

Take a paper rectangle, 2 inches by 6 inches long, and cut a 3-inch slit down the middle. Fold the two flaps down in opposite directions. At the other end, twist the paper into a tight roll. Hold the mini-helicopter high above your head and watch it twirl to the ground.

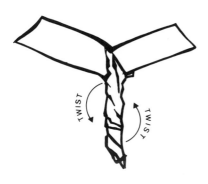

Outdoor Challenge 3.

Find out which "animal" year you were born in, according to this 12-year Chinese calendar. When the Year of the Pig is over, the cycle begins again with the Year of the Rat. To find out the "animal" year for a person whose birth year does not appear here, start adding 12 to the birth year until you see a year on this wheel. For instance, if your mother was born in 1960, add 12. Then you're at 1972, which turns out to be the Year of the Rat.

Outdoor Challenge 2.

Ask your friend to stand with one side of his or her body against a wall. Your friend's ear, arm and foot should touch the wall. Now it is impossible for your friend to lift the outside foot!

Outdoor Challenge 4.

In general, if you see the moon in the evening hours, it is getting bigger (waxing). It is getting smaller (waning), if you see it in the morning hours. Try another test — look at the dark part of the moon. Is it on the left? If it is, then the moon is waxing. If it is on the right, then the moon is waning. This test must be reversed in the Southern Hemisphere, and won't work near the equator!

Continued from page 125:

8. No resting or hiding places for fish here! Also, no shade to keep the water cool. **9.** (See 3.) **10.** Little fish are food for big fish. **11.** Sometimes the machinery in the plant doesn't work properly and excess sewage flows into the lake. **12.** Even though most fish will not come across the pipe given the size of the lake, some fish are sucked in every day.

Photograph Credits

Mike Assaly: pages 2, 111.

Ray Boudreau: front cover; pages 1, 3, 4–5, 7, 8–9, 10, 11, 12–13, 15, 16, 17, 18, 19, 20–21, 22–23, 25, 26, 28, 29, 31, 32–33, 34–35, 37, 39, 40–41, 42–43, 48, 50–51, 52, 55, 57, 60–61, 63, 65, 68–69, 71, 72–73, 75, 76–77, 78–79, 80, 84–85, 86–87, 88–89, 90–91, 95, 97, 102–103, 107, 110, 112–113, 118–119, 121, 122–123; back cover.

Nigel Dickson: cover (center), pages 45, 63.

Matthew Levin: pages 67, 82–83.

Hal Roth: pages 60, 61.

Tony Thomas: pages 4–5 (bottom left), 44, 47, 49, 56, 59, 93, 100–101, 104–105, 108–109, 114–115.

Peter Walker: page 99.

Ron Watts: page 41.

Illustration Credits

Josephine Cheng: pages 8, 9, 10, 11, 12, 13, 19, 22, 24, 25, 26, 28, 29.

Julie Colantonio: pages 72–73, 101, 114, 126.

Anita Granger: pages 46, 66.

Dan Hobbs: pages 92–93.

Tina Holdcroft: pages 104–105, 106–107.

Vesna Krstanovich: pages 7, 14, 17, 20, 27, 30, 34, 35, 81, 94, 116–117.

San Murata: pages 124–125.

Joe Weissman: 38.

If you've had fun reading **The Anti-Boredom Book**, here's a selection of other Owl Books you'll also enjoy!

For kids aged 3–8

- **Baby Science: How Babies _Really_ Work!** by Ann Douglas
- **Science Fun** by Gordon Penrose
- The **Amazing Things Animals Do** series by Marilyn Baillie
- **Two Dozen Dinosaurs** by Catherine Ripley
- The **Owl Mini-Book** series by the editors of _Owl_ magazine
- The **I Can Make** series by Mary Wallace

For kids aged 7–12

- **The Family Tree Detective: Cracking the Case of Your Family's Story** by Ann Douglas
- **You Asked? Over 300 Great Questions and Astounding Answers** by the editors of _Owl_ magazine
- **Scary Science: The Truth Behind Vampires, Witches, UFOs, Ghosts and More** by Sylvia Funston
- **Crime Science: How Investigators Use Science to Track Down the Bad Guys** by Vivien Bowers
- **Cartooning for Kids** by Marge Lightfoot
- **The Science Explorers** series by Elin Kelsey

Look for these award-winning Owl titles, and others, at your neighborhood or on-line bookstore.